34443001013434

133.9
Quinn   Quinn, Gary

May the angels be
with you

DUE DATE

		.	

May the Angels
Be with You

May the Angels Be with You

A Psychic Helps You
Find Your Spirit Guides
and Your True Purpose

Gary Quinn

Harmony Books
New York

To our higher angels and guides
who are always there to give love and information
for each individual, so that they
may create heaven on earth

Copyright © 2001 by Gary Quinn

Published by Harmony Books, New York, New York.
Member of the Crown Publishing Group.

Random House, Inc. New York, Toronto, London, Sydney, Auckland
www.randomhouse.com

Harmony Books is a registered trademark and the Harmony Books colophon
is a trademark of Random House, Inc.

Printed in the United States of America

Design by Susan Maksuta

Library of Congress Cataloging-in-Publication Data
Quinn, Gary.
May the angels be with you : a psychic helps you find your
spirit guides and your true purpose / by Gary Quinn.—1st ed.
1. Guides (Spiritualism)   2. Guardian angels.   I. Title.
BF1275.G85 Q56 2001
133.9—dc21
00-049874

ISBN 0-609-60804-5

10 9 8 7 6 5 4 3 2 1

First Edition

CONTENTS

CONTENTS

INTRODUCTION
Expect Help

The journey you are about to embark on in this book will take you many places you've never been before. You will feel a wide range of emotions, come upon worlds of possibility you never realized were open to you, and investigate places in your soul that call out for investigation. You will slowly develop the certainty—not just the faith or hope—that guidance is yours for the asking.

Seem like an impossible promise? It certainly sounds as if such a trip—like the Grand Tour rich people used to take a century or more ago—will require all kinds of preparation: packing clothes for every occasion and climate, getting all necessary shots to ward off disease, learning many different languages, obtaining visas and passports, preparing to leave home for a long duration. It sounds exciting, perhaps, but maybe more than you feel you're up to.

However well intentioned they are, many "spiritual" books, and in particular books about angels, often make it seem that the meditative adventure they describe and advocate is as complicated as that aforementioned Grand Tour. You are sometimes deluged with arcane details about cosmology—about how the Universe "really" works— about the hierarchy of heavenly (and not so heavenly) spiritual or "divine" beings. The very specificity of these approaches may at first appear to lend credibility to their claims: how could so much be known if it weren't on some level "true"?

Without in any way desiring to debunk these claims, I'd like to offer a note of reassurance, here at the start, that you don't have to acquire complicated visas and passports or learn unfamiliar languages to enter the realm to which this book invites you. As Dorothy discovered, Oz (despite all its wonders, beauties, mysteries, and miracles) had nothing on Kansas. She'd always had everything she needed right at home. She just hadn't known it before.

If you question that payoff, you're not alone. Oz has all that magic, color, suspense, and fun—flying monkeys, a wizard, a talking scarecrow, a tin man, a cowardly lion, gleaming emerald towers, apple trees that throw apples, a good witch in a floating bubble, and a green-colored cackling bad one on a broom—and what Dorothy gets is more brown farm dirt? What kind of trade-off is that? Seems more like a cruel trick.

Actually, Kansas wasn't Dorothy's prize any more than Oz was. The prize was her ability to envision the most marvelous dream she could imagine and then find ways to explore it, live in it, overcome her fear of it, love it—and learn from it that there were many Ozzes and Kansases, as many as she felt like creating. We tend to regard the circumstances we were born with or into (parents, genetic inheritance, wealth or lack thereof, siblings, where we were born, education, size of nose, color of hair, and so on) as a prison sentence: we feel as trapped as Dorothy once did in Kansas and even (before she realized she could exit the dream anytime she wanted to) in Oz.

But we're not trapped. Limitations, like fears, are illusions. Miracles are not illusions: they are part of the basic fabric of our lives. It is one of the primary missions of this book to help you understand just how free you really are and how normal miracles are. Not by lecturing you, but by beckoning to you to open up and discover all this for yourself.

The world is spread out before you like a feast. How do you see that feast, partake of what's in it?

Expect to. Expect that the feast is there and that it's there for you. That's the simple "trick." I'll enlarge the invitation. *Expect help.* You will learn that this does not mean "expect help sometime in the future when some source of it is ready to bestow it." Expect help now. Help is being offered to you now. Help has always been offered to you.

All it takes to realize the simplicity of this great universal truth is to calm down and let the possibility in. As you'll see in the following pages, you need only to "act as if." (We'll give that a good deal of play later on; let me just plant the seed of it now.)

Thoughts have tremendous power. We are continually in the process of creating ourselves every moment we breathe, every moment we act from our assumptions and perceptions of the world. The cliché "you know a man from the company he keeps" is profoundly true—but doesn't begin to tell the half of it. You know a human being from every manifestation of his or her life. This fact suggests an often unnerving—and after you've recovered from the shock of seeing your complicity in it—sometimes rueful irony.

The questions most clients come to me wanting to ask are usually very basic: "How can I make more money, find the right relationship, be the success I want to be? *How can I get what I want?*" In a way, a perfectly plausible answer (here comes that irony) is: "Just keep doing what you're doing. Because whether you know it or not, you've been creating the world that some unconscious part of you thinks you deserve all along. It wouldn't be your world otherwise."

How do you stop this unwitting self-sabotage? The answer is first to become aware of the thought-to-reality mechanism that is already at work in your life, but over which you haven't yet learned to exert control. In other words, to be who you want to be, to have the life you want to have, you first have to examine your motives. You have to be sure you're sending out to the world the clearest, most examined, and most honest intentions you're capable of conveying. All of us are already manifesting our desires, and if we're not happy with their outcome, we'll benefit by becoming more conscious of the motives we're really working from. Then we can focus on changing them so that we *do* get what we want. This usually means acknowledging assumptions that have been holding us back because we haven't completely registered that we have them—for example, that you don't deserve what you desire, that risk-taking is too terrifying to attempt safely, and/or that you have to do it all yourself.

Let's quickly debunk the last of these misguided and self-impeding assumptions (we'll deal with the other two later on): the idea that "you have to do it all yourself."

In two words, you don't. In fact, in two other words, you can't! If you knew how much you already have been helped, and are being helped right now, any fantasy that you're a lone wolf crying in the wilderness would evaporate like the mist it is.

This book is about angels. But it's also about the infinite interconnectedness of the spiritual and the material realms we all inhabit, the infinite joyful abundance of the Universe, and the infinite help that is available to you to become exactly who you want to be.

Keep it simple. All you have to do is ask, with a clear heart and an open spirit, for what you want.

You know what the first result will be? A resounding cheer from the whole angelic realm: *"Hooray! You've figured out the secret!"* Imagine all these angels eagerly poised for flight, awaiting only the barest invitation from you to soar into your life.

1

HANG ON FOR THE RIDE

Angel came down from heaven yesterday.

Stayed with me just long enough to rescue me...

These words from a half-remembered Carlos Santana song darted from somewhere into my groggy head and nudged me out of my nap on the plane from L.A., beckoned me to open my eyes, pulled at me to feast on the visual splendor of Sun Valley, Idaho, now dawning below. Like sentries on the road to a royal banquet, great jagged outcrops of boulder and rock framed the city's spread.

I began to sense the miracle from the moment the plane touched ground: the very air was magic. I knew this was someplace I was supposed to be. More words rang in my head: *"A table has been prepared!"*

I was clear about what I had been invited to provide at that "table": two presentations covering one topic, "How to Contact Your Angels." I had prepared for these talks in my usual way—amassing notes, stories, anecdotes, and meditations, the joyful spillover from my lifelong absorption in the power and guidance of angels. I also looked forward to giving as many one-on-one "angel readings" as time and energy would permit. The venue was the Third Annual Sun Valley Wellness Festival at the Elkhorn Resort Lodge, whose organizer, Liz Caldwell, had known my work in L.A. as a psychic counselor and "angel channeler" and had invited me to share my experience with the large and varied group who had come to expand their spiritual lives.

Arriving at the resort, I felt embraced by both place and people; already my spirit was being fed. During the guided meditation with which I opened my first talk, I quickly sensed in the packed room the ebullient energy of many souls at various stages of receptivity "going with me," all of them eager to explore whatever opportunities this encounter might provide them. It was as if a joyful convocation of souls—a "soul party"—had spontaneously formed around me.

As I led my Sun Valley group in this meditation introducing them to the Seven Angels that we would investigate throughout our time together, beckoning them to let go of their fear and resistance, I sensed a softening, a collective opening of hearts in the room. I felt the imminent prospect of widespread healing and the certainty that it would be fostered here. An overpowering sense of the Universe's abundance flooded through me. I knew that all we ever needed to do was let that abundance in—and shed as many of our assumptions and expectations as we could. I knew—and I prayed to help every soul in the room also to realize—that the rewards of letting go will always, always turn out to be incalculably greater than any of us dream.

All of my carefully compiled notes, all of the prep work I'd done for the seminar, probably had some subliminal benefit to me when I got up to speak for the several-hour sessions I conducted each day. But I can't remember looking at my notebook. Something magical and transcendent took over—I spoke and listened without any hesitation or self-consciousness. The angels I channel privately in my practice now came fully, freely, abundantly to my aid. So many memories of faces at Sun Valley stay with me: the woman whose son had recently died—his name (Michael) and nickname (Bo) came to me the moment I saw her—and her stunned and grateful expression as I passed on his message of love and peace and hope to her is something I shall never forget. Other men and women began to sense the presence of their guardian angels, sometimes visually, more often registering them internally—in a remembered dream, song, poem. So many connections were made within, between, and among everyone, all strengthening my understanding that I was *not* the source of any of them. I had simply enabled these people to connect with each other and with their own higher selves and at least some sense of angelic guidance. All I have been and can ever be is a conduit, a channel, through which information and guidance can flow. This gives my life its purpose—at every moment I'm grateful for the gift of being able to provide this angelic "phone line." But it is a gift whose ultimate aim is to become unnecessary. My goal is to let everyone know that angelic love and guidance are available to all of us, right now. All you have to do is let it in. You don't need a channeler for this. (But I'll be here until you realize you don't.) My Sun Valley experience helped me to connect profoundly to this mission once again.

This goal is the book's mission, too: to help you let angelic wisdom into your life and heart. If you had even the slightest inkling how completely and powerfully you are loved by the angels around you, you would cry for joy—and then quickly become reassured that you had all the resources, so many more than you ever dreamed you had, to turn your life into the magnificent adventure you want it to be.

THE SOUL PARTY

I resort to using the word *abundant* so often in describing angels because it suggests their great teeming variety and energy—but what word can really capture how wild, light, infinite, joyful, and expansive their presence is? Language is too linear for this task; words tell you only how A connects to B connects to C. The realm of angels is timeless, rich, multidimensional, with levels of meaning you have to feel to understand. The only way I know to begin to understand the nature of this realm is simply to allow ourselves to feel its impact and influence and love. All any of us has to do is give up our resistance to receiving this influence. Angels have so much to tell us. And we can benefit so profoundly from what they want to teach us. The very world would heal if, collectively, "it"—we—learned to heed their call.

But remember it's a "soul party"! At one point I tried to describe to my group what it's like to receive angelic help: "Think of it as a ride in Disneyland!" Angels are messengers of joy. They are not the washed-out, faintly smiling, dull little icons you see in cliché religious art. They are as delightful, ingenious, and exciting as they are infinitely loving. They are one with their happy, urgent messages. They are pure focused bursts of joy. In fact, you're not fully "hearing" an angel if something inside you doesn't feel like it's positively glowing.

How do I know this? What's my proof?

I have never been bothered by the question of "proof" with regard to spiritual phenomena. To me, if something is true, it will eventually reveal itself as true. You don't have to go scrambling after it. If you have the human optical ability to see color, and you are taught the names of different colors, no one will have to prove to you that (on clear June days) the sky is blue. Truth is self-evident. So it is with angels: if you allow them into your heart, mind, and life, angels will help you to transform your life. Ask them for help with this transformation, and see what happens.

If you truly have cleared the way for their entry, you'll have more proof of their power, love, and truth than any argument anyone could pose. The proof is in the experience—and the experience awaits you whenever you want it.

Not that we don't sometimes go to extraordinary lengths to blind ourselves to truth. Human history largely documents this kind of willful blindness and denial—blindness and denial fueled by fear, which is perhaps truth's worst enemy. Eventually, with your angels' help, you'll see that all fear is illusion. In fact, you might want to start to chant these four words to yourself—"Fear is a lie"—even if you can't quite yet bring yourself to believe it. Eventually the truth of it will prove itself.

Spiritual or religious defensiveness has always struck me as sad and self-defeating—not only when people are determinedly closed off from experiencing anything other than the material world, but also when a proponent of a particular spiritual "truth" attempts to cram it down someone else's throat. There hasn't been a religious pundit yet who through sheer force of "logic" was able to sway any nonbeliever one iota toward an alien belief. Truth will out, if only we'll learn to get out of its way. I don't have to lecture you on the blueness of the sky. All you need to do is look up at it.

So right off, please understand that this book neither defends nor attacks any particular view (religious or otherwise) of angels. I have no angelic "ax" to grind. I do only what I know how to do: pass on "the news" that these miraculous beings in various ways pass on to me. Their truth—or the truth of this or that speculation I make based on what they tell me—will speak to you or it won't. If it does, all the "proof" I'm interested in is that it's helping you. If it doesn't, well—there's always its entertainment value! (But don't give up on it quite yet.)

Letting go of our defenses is frightening at first—but ultimately it is such a relief! I urge you to try to release your fear and anger every chance you get, especially any moment you feel yourself clench and about to say, "But..." Allow whatever feeling, thought, or opinion occurs to you simply to be. Just "hear" it. Don't argue or attempt to explain it away. Don't do anything about it! Simply make room for whatever thoughts come after it. Entertain each of your thoughts, like guests. Be courteous, withhold judgment, just keep the flow going. Eventually it will become clear to you which "guests" feel welcome (or "true"). You will be clearing your psychic airwaves—not only to allow truth to reveal and prove itself, but also to open up the path for your angels.

Experiencing the presence of angels is enlivening, abundant, rich, a little like listening in on the spiritual radio waves of the world: cliff-hanger stories, ringing laughter, miraculous solutions, deeply loving support. Perhaps this all sounds a bit frantic, but it isn't at all. Angelic peace proceeds from a perfect unconditional love—a stillness somewhere mysteriously within the angel—that answers to something just as deep in ourselves. There may well be joyous and productive activity at the "surface" of this peace, but there's always a stillness at its heart.

WHAT ANGELS ARE—AND AREN'T

Many people envision angels as little pink winged humanoids whose wan smiles too rarely engage much interest or curiosity. As a result, even if we profess to believe in them, we often envision our "guardian angels" (and we do all have guardian angels) as comfortingly dependable icons, like caricatures of perfect aunts, grandparents, uncles. We may also feel—or crave to believe—that any angels who may be helping us are the souls of recently departed loved ones. The pain of loss often induces the hope that they are by our side spiritually now, as angels.

Departed souls can have a great, loving, and beneficial impact on our lives: you may well feel the presence of loved ones who've passed on. But their gifts emanate from human souls in transition from one state of being to another. Their guidance is very personal, invested with a lifetime of particular lessons and caring, a focused attention we can receive from no one else. Angels are not human—and therefore have no human past to distract or prejudice them. They invite deep trust and intimacy, but their primary function is to convey whatever particular joyful messages we need to thrive. They are infinitely adaptable and full of quicksilver ingenuity and transformations, and yet there is something changeless in their being, in the constancy of their unconditional love for us. They are what and where they are meant to be: accessible to human consciousness, and connected to spiritual realms we cannot reach without their help. Their place in both divine and human realms is securely set.

I bring up the distinction between angels and departed human souls for one very practical reason. I had a number of (initially bewildering) encounters with various spiritual presences, not all of them (I learned) worth embracing or listening to. In other words, I learned that not every voice in my head is an angel.

This doesn't mean that some sinister Addams Family ghouls are out there to get you. Each of us has the inborn capacity to tell "good" spiritual influence from "bad." Distressing spirits are almost always those of departed souls who have not yet made the full transition from the physical realm to the spiritual; their anxiety and fear get passed on to whoever is receptive to it. There is always a note of despair or anger or bitterness in our experience of these souls. You feel more troubled than helped by your encounter with them. But to disengage, you have only to say and feel no to them. It's that simple.

Angels, on the other hand, are infinitely joyful and loving. While an encounter with an angel may unnerve you a bit (indeed, it often will), it's always because the angel is beckoning you to achieve something more joyful, rewarding, pleasurable, and/or ambitious than you previously dared to consider taking on. Feelings of love and support with angels always increase, never decrease. There isn't the barest touch of negativity in any angelic presence: there is only joy.

Each of us has the spiritual equivalent of what Hemingway described as a writer's most valuable tool: a "crap detector." If, down in your gut or in your subtlest inner ear, something you hear or think feels even a little forced or fake, or in some other way just "doesn't work," it's very likely "crap." Ditto spiritual impressions, especially if they're touched by anxiety or other distress. Cut yourself off from the source of this negative emanation quickly and completely. (This is an instance where "Just say no" really works.) Once again, if the spiritual or psychic message or feeling is "true" or angelic in origin, you'll know it. If it's not, you'll know it, too: it will tend to claw you in the gut.

Of course, if truth were always so easy to perceive and acknowledge, a lot more would be self-evident. Certainly if the truth about angels came to us more frequently in physically or conventionally identifiable ways, we wouldn't have consigned them to Christmas decorations or wishful sitcoms. We would acknowledge them openly in our lives as very real presences.

But we learn some truths slowly. In fact, perhaps all important truths are understood only by degree. I think of my own childhood and the strange eruption of psychic images and feelings and thoughts I had even as a child—experiences that, when I discovered they were by no means widely shared, I often tried to cover up. I felt that my psychic ability was an affliction, an annoying (if sometimes useful, even lucrative) blip on my mental screen that would more likely end me up in the loony bin than on the Leno show. It set me apart. It was unnerving. I didn't always want to know what I knew.

MY STORY

I've always been sensitive to energies around me—from earliest childhood I was aware of various presences I felt but could not see. Sometimes they were negative, sometimes positive. I learned to keep most of these impressions to myself. I remember looking at a child in elementary school and knowing he would die young—and not too many years later, he did. I would be taken places by my family and see colors and auras around people—it was some time before I found out that not everyone sees what I later learned were these spiritual entities. Once, visiting my step-grandmother in Tennessee with my family, I fell asleep in an upstairs room and woke to feel two hands on my throat! The next morning this woman spoke of her husband who had recently died in the house: it was clear that it had been his distressed spirit I had encountered. I told no one about these events except my sister, whom I could trust to keep it to herself.

Through my teens I sometimes made comments or predictions to my mother about other people we knew or I had seen and later learned they turned out to be true. But I never experienced these premonitions and intuitions as a gift or useful ability. They were something, rather, to escape when I could. One means of escape was swimming. It was a lifesaver to me. We moved so much when I was a child that I never had any real secure sense of home or place: swimming was something I could do anywhere, something that soothed me, allowed me to enter a kind of trance—I realize now it was one of my first modes of meditation. Supposedly "unbearable" sets of 2,000 yards at a time were nothing to me. I was at this time studying with Sherm Chavoor, who had trained such great athletes as Mark Spitz, Debbie Meyer, and Mike Burton. I'd found something for which I had a natural aptitude, but one of its greatest pleasures was that it enabled me to tune out. I'd swim for 4 1/2 to 5 hours a day and feel myself "leave," sometimes so completely that after practice when I went to school, teachers would stop me in the hall and attempt to flag me down: "Hello, Gary! Where are you?" It sounds funny now— I'm sure I did often come across as a space cadet—but I realize now that I *was* truly going somewhere else, to some psychic "space" that was inside me and outside "normal" perception of the world. It was as if the meditative and psychic ability that I had tried to dismiss were creating a life of its own: since I seemed to refuse to direct it, it was pulling me. I wasn't aware then how often and readily I'd learned to leave my body. All I knew is that when I swam, meditatively "checking out" was as natural to me as breathing. Little did I know that I was opening the channels in myself for future psychic work and revelation.

I was not completely disconnected from the "real world." As I grew older, I would have a thought about or see a picture of this or that celebrity—and then look up to see the very person in front of me! At UCLA, various story ideas for the then-current hit sitcom *Laverne & Shirley* came to me almost like dreams—and within days of this "vision," I found myself meeting one of the show's stars, Penny Marshall, and her husband, Rob Reiner, at the celebrity sports event *Battle of the Network Stars* in Mission Viejo, and shortly thereafter becoming the youngest staff writer on the show. While living in Los Angeles undoubtedly increases one's chances of meeting "show business" personalities—celebrity is a kind of Los Angeles industry, after all—my various encounters, collaborations, brief meetings, and/or friendships with Henry Winkler and Erin Moran (on the neighboring set of *Happy Days;* Erin and I did a mean imitation of Sonny and Cher doing "I Got You Babe"), Farrah Fawcett, Stefanie Powers, Flip Wilson, Phyllis George, Carrie Fisher, Teri Garr, Carol Kane, Marilu Henner, Lucille Ball, and Milton Berle all transpired during this period not because I was a name-dropping celebrity hound but simply because on some deep soul level, I "wanted" to meet them. I had stumbled onto a power I now know that we all have: we always manifest whatever we truly desire. *Truly* is, however, the operative word: because we often manifest what we secretly, unconsciously expect or believe we deserve (not what we may tell ourselves or other people we want), this revelation is not always a happy one. Only later did I realize how completely we *all* create our lives and how what we truly desire always, inevitably manifests. Getting control of this amazing psychic faculty therefore means becoming conscious of our secret fears and desires so that we can see what the real motivating force is in our lives. Only then can we begin to exert some kind of control over how that force manifests. (We'll deal with that crucial task throughout this book.)

However unwittingly I had trained myself to see and begin to exploit this connection in my life—all those years of meditative swimming had a lot to do with it—by the time I was in my early twenties, I knew that I had an ability to summon up the people and experiences I most longed for or needed to have in my life. If I wanted it with clear vision and a pure heart, I would have it. It was really that simple.

I must also have "truly desired" a spiritual education at this point because I began to be drawn to, and study with, various spiritual teachers and guides—first among them, the Reverend Polette Carabel. It was in her house that I first felt the vibrations of angels. She enabled me to "regress" to various previous lives that made clear what "karma" (life experience) I had to address in this life. I always wondered why I had met and worked with so many actresses: now I learned that in a previous life, I had been a priest ministering to various powerful women, and that my life in L.A. was in some ways the product and continuation of that legacy.

First working as assistant to various stars, I eventually became an actor's manager—and I began to be known as "that psychic agent." I was already starting to "channel" information that helped other people progress in their careers or look at what they needed to move forward. I knew from the start that I was not the source of any great wisdom: I was simply the channel through which this information could be imparted to others. I often didn't remember what I'd said to people whom I "read": it didn't matter that *I* got the information, it only mattered that it was passed on to the person whom it was intended to help.

And then I went to Paris.

The opportunity came because a friend of mine, Michel, needed someone to help him out on an antique-buying expedition. I was happy to oblige. I'd had abundant experience organizing other people's lives—but to have the chance to do it in Paris! I leaped at the opportunity.

Emerging from the plane at Charles DeGaulle Airport was a revelation. From the moment my feet hit ground, I knew I belonged there. I knew France. In some fundamental way it was my home. I did not know the language—by no means had I ever been a "Francophile." This recognition went far deeper than that. The spirit of the place resonated with me. I was filled with the certainty that I had not only been here before but was here now for a reason. I knew I was in the right place at the right time.

Having this sense of certainty was exhilarating. But it was also ultimately useful psychic training. It increased my trust in my own intuitions, even those that beckoned me to take leaps into uncharted territory. And as much as I "knew" France in some deep psychic way, it was still very much uncharted territory to me. In addition to speaking no French, I didn't know anyone in the country, and I hadn't a clue what I'd come to learn or what I'd end up doing. I only knew that, whatever my purpose in France was, eventually it would reveal itself to me. All I had to do was what I was doing already: remain open, trust the urgings of my own heart—and hang on for the ride.

It was a magical trip: meeting Michel's friends and family (we stayed at the home of one of his parents in the exclusive Avenue Foch); connecting with a woman who would later be my lawyer and confidante, Maha Dib (both of us instantly understanding that we had known each other in past lives); even finding myself performing a song from *Grease* (in which I'd performed in L.A.) in the renowned Parisian club Le Palace, which led to the offer of a singing contract from a record executive (Maha's cousin) at Delphine Records. (Later, writing a song on the spot with a composer in a twenty-four-track studio and recording it, I discovered I was channeling a black blues singer I had known in a past life in New Orleans!) Talk about hanging on for the ride! Almost everything I saw, touched, tasted, heard, or smelled, everyone I met and spoke with, all not only had meaning to me but were occasions for joyful revelation. And all slowly deepened my sense of and trust in my psychic abilities—which I was finally able to identify as a gift, not an affliction.

Now I can cut to the chase. Walks alone around Paris, and a trip to visit friends in Rome, all strengthened my certainty that in some sense I had come back to Europe to rediscover how vital and strong my soul identity was. It was a way of learning to love and value myself, my karmic and past-life self, and my abilities and gifts in my current life. I think it is true that we cannot give or receive love until we have learned really to love ourselves. This was a lesson I didn't know I was learning at the time. But it became clearer to me when I finally visited Notre Dame.

When I entered the great old church, I sat down in a pew and allowed the place to "speak" to me. If I had felt I was "home" in France before, I knew I was home now. I lit a candle. I felt a welcoming vibration: a sense of rooted peace and rightness. I was definitely in the right place.

With the record contract in place, I felt as if I were being beckoned to put down roots in Paris. I needed to return to Los Angeles to clean up my life there—finish various tasks, tie up loose ends—but all with the wonderful glowing image of Paris ahead of me, and the certainty that I was meant to return—which I did the moment I'd finished in L.A. I'd put a good deal of trust in the recording contract that had come so miraculously to me from Delphine Records: I was sure that it would mark the beginning of my real Parisian life. But my first call to the company produced devastating news. I was told the contract would not pan out. It had been canceled.

What was I going to do? I'd come back to Paris with little money, banking on the deal I thought I'd made with Delphine Records. Now the whole plan—and my hopes of security—just vanished into air. I was in a complete tailspin, desperate for guidance. I returned to Notre Dame every day for three weeks and prayed for some sign about what I should do next. Why had I been so sure that France was the right place for me when now, suddenly, nothing was working out? Could I have been that mistaken?

Then, on the third day of the third week, I experienced a life-changing revelatory vision. I sat alone in a pew—there was no one else in the church except for an old woman praying in a corner. It was unusual for the cathedral to be so empty on a beautiful April day at three P.M. But all was quiet. Something beckoned me to look up. From the ceiling of Notre Dame, a brilliant vortex of purple light flowed down onto me, bathing me—twinkling around me in a dance, I suddenly saw, of five to seven angels! They whirled around my face and spoke to me telepathically. They told me to trust my journey to France: I was supposed to be here. My guardian angel, the Archangel Michael, made himself known to me, speaking his name. He continued to reassure me that I'd be all right. I was anxious because I had almost no money and would not be able to stay with my friends for longer than a week. But this angelic energy was amazing—warm, buoyant, strong—holding me up like a wave of calm.

I walked back to my apartment. As soon as I entered it, the phone rang: a friend of mine, Xavier, was calling to tell me I had a free place to stay if I wanted it. The rest of my trip in France similarly sorted itself out like dominoes falling at exactly the right moment, in exactly the right direction. It was clear to me that I was not in France to work (the reason I'd thought I'd come there) but rather to learn principles of love and trust—and to feed, cultivate, and reinforce them by regularly turning to and appealing for help from my guides.

Since then the new deep sense of peace that my angels bestowed in my heart has completely transformed my life. I knew these angels were revealing themselves to me because I had finally become receptive to them—I had opened my heart and trusted that I would be guided and cared for. They gave me more than reassurance about being in France, more than a sense that I was starting to follow the path in my life that I was meant to follow. They did more than banish my fears and doubts. I knew in some way they were preparing me for the next important step in my life.

They were readying me for my life's work, which I had finally become ready to understand and embrace. The purpose of my being in France, of my returning to Notre Dame, was now clear to me. These eager loving angels needed my help—just as they need yours, all of our help. They wanted me to spread the word. Healing—joy—enlightenment—fulfillment—exaltation—purpose—love: all these yearned-for states of being are so much more available to most people than they know. All most of us need is a nudge to wake up, open our eyes—see, trust in, and begin to make use of the infinite guidance and love that these angels so ardently want us to enjoy.

I now knew they wanted me to help provide that nudge. I wouldn't have to proselytize or bang any drums. All I'd have to do is what I'm doing now: stay open, pass on what I receive to you, and pray that you'll hang on for the ride.

The angels will take care of the rest.

2

CLEARING THE WAY
How to Tap into "Angel Power"
(Even If You Don't Believe in Angels!)

The lessons that help us in life seem to come not only because we need them but because we're receptive to them. Certainly this is how the knowledge of my own guardian angels came to me. You've seen the growth of my own receptivity in the story I've just told you. As a child, my psychic gift seemed to come from nowhere—it was bewildering to me that others didn't sense or know the things that I sensed and knew. Learning that my ability to foresee certain aspects of the future or know what others were thinking seemed "abnormal" to others, I generally kept this psychic ability secret. Understanding and accepting the nature of this "gift" took many years. Part of my education came almost by default: I began to realize that when my psychic energies were not focused, they often seemed to turn from gift to curse! When I feel scattered, uncentered, and out of touch with the still quiet voice inside me, computers and fax machines near me malfunction; lightbulbs go out; a kind of chaos seems to erupt about me. But as I quiet down and make contact again with my angels' guidance within me, as I again trust and rely on the gift of being able to "hear" them, things get better. The more I am able to achieve and sustain a meditative receptive state, the clearer my own path becomes. It was this kind of greater receptivity that I described in Notre Dame, when the source of my psychic gift first made itself known to me. Angels flowed down toward me in that glowing column of purplish light *because something in me was ready*—at that moment—to see them, receive them.

Why did they choose that *particular* moment to come—not an hour before, or a week after? After all, I had returned to Notre Dame every day for three weeks and prayed for guidance: why hadn't my epiphany come sooner? Actually, it was only when I *stopped* praying in an urgent way for particular guidance—when I was able to *let go* of my preconceived notions of what guidance "ought" to be—that help freely flooded in. My angels became visible to me, and I experienced a profound and overwhelming sense of serenity, love, hope—and a definite notion of the next "right" thing to do—because I had given them a kind of clear "landing pad." I wasn't blocking them with my own fearful requirements or urgencies. I simply let myself be who I was, with no expectations and no demands. Or to use the word I often use with my clients, I gave myself *permission* just to be—and to believe and affirm that I deserved as much of the infinite abundance available to all of us as I could take in. That was when my life opened up, and—as if in a chain of dominoes—miracles started to occur in my life. Material prosperity, friends, spiritual and professional connections, my growing practice as a psychic counselor—all of these became available as soon as I became clear enough to let them in. As long as I let myself *be,* with no preconceptions of what I was "supposed" to be, my angels would make their guidance known most clearly, and my life would flourish.

This receptivity, this ability to "let go" so that we can take full advantage of our angels' help, will always grow and deepen if we let it. Our capacity to receive the abundance of the universe never stops—there are always new adventures, opportunities, and revelations as long as we continue to stay open. My knowledge of who my guardian angel specifically is seems to have come to me only because I had "let go" on yet a deeper level. It was when I let go and took the leap—made the decision to devote my life to using my psychic gift to counsel people, made the full-time commitment to help others as my main task on this planet—that the identity of my guardian angel (the Archangel Michael) became known to me. In other words, it was only when *I began to do what I truly was on this earth to do*—help other people to become more aware of their own angels' presence, love, help, and guidance—that my own path became clear. This is a lesson my clients have learned again and again. The more they permit themselves (with their angels' guidance) to become more of *who they truly are*—the more they embrace their higher selves and follow the simple still voice inside them that leads them to their truest path in life—the more quickly and fully their lives blossom and their happiness and serenity grow.

Even if (as is often the case) my clients do not and perhaps never are able to "see" or identify their angels the way I had been allowed to see mine, they are still helped by them. As a reader and counselor in a client's presence, I can gently hold a "conference" between my angels and their angels and act as a conduit for their guardian angels' guidance. But that guidance is available to my clients—and is available to you—whether or not I or some other psychic "channel" act as the go-between. It is simply a matter of teaching ourselves, clearing the way, to receive it.

The good news is, you don't have to "believe" in angels in order to be helped by them. I ask you right now to accept on faith that they are with you every moment of your life, gently encouraging you, attempting to help you every step of the way, no matter what you believe or don't believe about their existence. All we seem to have to do to be flooded with their abundant loving guidance is to learn how to "clear the decks" for it to arrive. And we seem to clear the decks best by acting "as if" our angels exist—simply taking it on faith that they do.

THE MAGIC WORDS: "AS IF..."

Acting "as if" isn't as hard as it may appear: each one of us as children did it all the time. It's what grown-ups call "play," and it is often the way children receive their angels' guidance very early on. It is natural for a child to "make believe"—to create whole new worlds of dreams and possibility and to live in them "as if" they existed. In fact, for the moment, these "as if" realms *do* exist—bark, maple leaves, and mud pies become a royal harvest feast, oak trees in the backyard become an enchanted forest, a Little League baseball diamond becomes Yankee Stadium, gleaming broken shells at the beach become precious jewels. Children move freely between imagination and physical reality—the two realms are fully and completely connected. But we are quickly educated to mistrust the imagination part of our experience—to dismiss what we "pretend" or "make up" as unreal. We are taught to believe only what we can see or prove in the "actual" physical world. We slowly lose our knowledge of the wonderful connection between the spiritual and the material worlds—a connection our angels can help us to reestablish and make use of as joyously as we did in play as children.

It's natural to be skeptical of this. The idea "if you can't see it, it doesn't exist" is one in which we've all been indoctrinated. But it's surprisingly simple to get beyond this resistance. Even my most skeptical clients—the ones who sneered most openly at the idea that "angels" had anything to do with their lives or their prospects for happiness—are now often able, virtually instantly, to dispel their cynicism by permitting themselves to act "as if" their angels did exist. All they've had to do is relearn what once came so naturally to them as children: to *let go and play.* Angels have an opening when we "play": when we're relaxed and imaginative, we're less defensive and guarded—and what begins as "pretend" can turn into a spiritual awakening. "Pretending" may sound like deception, but in fact it's really employing the playful childlike technique of "make believe" to open up your senses, mind, heart, and soul. Miracles can happen—in fact, *will* happen—when this opening occurs.

The power of "playing" is most movingly evident in clients of mine who come to me in a state of complete devastation—sometimes broke, jobless, and on the verge of losing home, car, and friends. Grace, 37 years old, was one of these self-described "failures." She had hoped to parlay a series of temp jobs working in advertising into a career—but there were always problems with bosses or coworkers, or she didn't agree with the politics of the company, or she'd had a bad bout of the flu—her disasters went on and on. Finally she lost her last job. But the deeper and more miserable question was that she really hadn't any idea what she wanted to do with her life, much less what she "should" do with it. She came to me as a last resort—she didn't have much truck with "psychics," but she'd heard that I was helpful from various secondhand sources, and since she was at the end of her rope, she thought she'd give me a try. She was knotted with tension when she first came to see me—her face tightly drawn, her clothes haphazardly worn, her hair lank and uncared for, her body movements frightened and tentative: she was the picture of a locked-up woman.

I invited Grace to sit down across from me and asked her to breathe deeply for a while. I asked her to let go of everything she had ever learned in the past. I asked her to calm her mind and to connect to the higher forces within her. She was so desperate for guidance, she followed my instructions with surprisingly little resistance—it was as if she were grateful to be told, like a child, "what to do." As she calmed herself into a meditative state, I asked her to visualize her angels. I assured her that she had two guardian angels who were always with her and whose whole task was to help her become a fully realized woman. I said: "I give you permission to be a success. You *are* a success already. The Universe is unlimited, flowing, abundant: it is already giving you everything you need. See yourself as already having everything you want. Give *yourself* permission to take all you want from this abundance. Put yourself in a satisfying and rewarding and lucrative job: see yourself in your new office doing what you love to do. Visualize yourself as having it now."

I told Grace various messages I was getting from her angels about opportunities that would open up in the next few days and weeks, but that it was up to her to take action—when these doors opened for her, she would have to walk through them. As I spoke, her body began to relax, a new lighter expression bloomed in her eyes, and the tension in her face softened. She was visibly letting in more of the Universe—right then and there—and while she was not able then to "see" or in any specific way register the presence of her guardian angels, she took my suggestion to ask them for guidance anyway—to simply act "as if" they were there because, I assured her, they *were* there. What she wanted and needed in her life was waiting for her; what she wanted wanted her, and her angels wanted to help her actively to attain it. She had only truly to believe that this was true, let go of her anxieties, and open her eyes to the phone calls she would get that would lead her to her next job—and take positive actions to improve her physical appearance so that it would reflect the beautiful woman and soul she already was.

This was the main message: *the abundance was already there.* Grace already had everything she needed to have the life she wanted. She only had to let go—stay alert—and follow up on the chances that would come her way. It became psychically clear to me that one of the most formidable resistances she was battling was the internalized voice of her mother, who had always berated her and told her she wasn't pretty and would never succeed at anything. I told her she could let go of that voice right then and there—that it had no more reality for her. Her whole demeanor softened and lightened more as she let that voice go. It was wonderful to see: as if her spirit were finally finding a way to free itself and breathe and enjoy the infinite abundance of life.

These words sound easy enough to say, but because they came from the deepest parts of me and answered the deepest needs in Grace, they had great power. In the next few days, Grace got the phone calls I had foreseen for her, and she soon landed a temp job that was in a field much closer to the one she wanted to enter. Because her attitude was different—and she was dressing with more self-care—her approach to work lightened and drew out more of her imagination and passion. Her mother's voice sometimes came back to haunt her, berate her in the old ways, but she had learned to quiet her mind and let the voice go—and to listen once again to that still inner voice inside all of us through which we truly hear our angels' guidance. What amazed her most was that her life was getting better, but not because she was "scheming" or in any way trying to force herself onto people—which is how she'd once thought professional success was attained. It was getting better because she was doing exactly the opposite: letting go of that control, and allowing life and opportunities to come to her. Grace is still not specifically aware of her angels—she does not see them or sense their individual presences in any direct way—but she asks for their guidance nonetheless. She has been able to find that "still soft inner voice" within her, and she trusts that it is the channel through which her guidance comes— which she still takes on "as if" faith as coming from her guardian angels—for a simple reason. Doing so helps her gain clarity, focus, and peace. Doing so works for her. "I don't need to see auras or spirits or winged cherubs flying above me to know that *something is guiding me*. I envision that 'something' as loving guidance from some entity or presence that cares about me because that's what it feels like. For now—and maybe forever—that's all I need to know. It's all the 'proof' I need that my angels are forever there and looking after me."

BE A UN AMBASSADOR

Anyone who takes the "as if" leap to believe in his or her guardian angels' beneficent help makes the remarkable discovery that the effect of this belief is a feeling of clarity, surrender, and receptivity: as Grace discovered, "success" is not a matter of straining to get something you think you "ought" to have. True success comes as a freely given gift—one that is full of opportunities that you must take action to bring into being, and one that comes to you unbidden. Grace got stuck from time to time in old negative tapes (for example, her mother's nagging criticism of her), which generally made her feel as if she had to take back the reins of her life and "do it all herself." That made her start to shut down again and become anxious, and lose her ability to hear that angel voice in the center of her. I suggested that she visualize herself as a UN ambassador hosting a gathering of other UN delegates, all of whom were simply invited to come in and "mingle" at the party. Her entire job was to greet the delegates and ambassadors as they entered the room and introduce those she knew to each other. All she had to do was open the door, let each of them in, and simply *be there:* be alert and warm, respond to people who came up to her to converse, but do nothing more than "facilitate" at the social event. I guaranteed her that in this vision everyone she wanted to meet would, at their own pace and in their own ways, come to her. Suggestions would be made, unanticipated invitations would be given, and unlooked-for opportunities would bloom like flowers in a garden. The world would open up for her. All she had to do to allow this opening was simply to *be there consciously.*

This vision is another way of describing the state of mind in which we can best hear the inner promptings that are our angels' guidance. But it is antithetical to most ideas of "getting ahead," especially in the corporate world. When I started my practice as a psychic counselor, most of my clients were actors and artists, many of them women— people who temperamentally were often more able to accept the suggestions of "letting go" and cultivating a meditative state so that they could locate the guiding voice their angels offered them than others who worked in fields like corporate finance. So it was interesting when, about a year and a half ago, a businessman in his early forties finally—very grudgingly—agreed to see me. He was doing so, he said, entirely at the urging of his wife, whom I had counseled over several months and who had sent all of their social circle to me as well: "Everyone I know goes to you, and my wife said I'd be crazy if I didn't try this out, but—well, I think I'm crazy because I *am* trying this out. I don't believe in any of this angel nonsense!"

Helping this man to relax and enter a meditative state where I could begin to "read" him—receive messages from his own guardian angels—was a daunting task. In fact, our first session was pretty much a disaster: his tension and resistance were so great that I only got bits and pieces of information, nothing that coalesced into anything that made much sense to him. As I explained in Chapter I, I am nothing but a channel for the information I receive: I often don't remember what I've said, because it's not actually "me" offering the communication—it's coming from a source outside me, a combination of the angels who surround my client and my own guardian angels who separately or collectively tell me what to say. But when a client is blocked, access to the source of his guidance is blocked, and we don't get very far. I was drained at the end of our first session with this man. I didn't feel I'd helped him at all. But when we were finished, I noticed that his shoulders had become less stiff—and there was, as there had been with Grace, a softer and more receptive look in his eyes. Evidently I had said that he had not sufficiently mourned his mother, whom I knew, from the partly blocked information I was getting, had recently died. I said that he needed to face and feel the emotions he was holding back about his loss—and also know that she was completely at peace and contented: he need not worry about her.

Amazingly (to me), this man insisted on coming back again the next week, and the next week after that—each week becoming more receptive to meditation, to "surrendering," to playing that UN ambassadorial "greeter"—and his life became happier at home, his business more expansive and successful. He now insists that all his colleagues consult me too, and he has become one of my most ardent champions.

I don't relate this story because of this gentleman's praise of me: as I've said, the information I impart doesn't come from me; it comes from a confluence of angel voices that communicate through me. The important point has to do with the simple but powerful emotional encounter this man was able to make with his own being—allowing himself (with me only as catalyst) to confront an emotional block that was stifling his personal life and interfering with his business judgments, so he could get beyond it. To this man, the idea of acting "as if" would have seemed the most childish nonsense before he had this emotional (which was for him also a spiritual) awakening. But now he happily, readily acts "as if" his angels are as real as I know them to be.

He prays to them for guidance. Like Grace, he has no particular or concrete sense of who or what they are: he only knows that appealing to them in a meditative state for help has widened and deepened his experience of life, allowed him to make more adventurous and profitable decisions in his career, and improved his marriage. "If it ain't broke, don't fix it" is pretty much his stance about his "as if" spirituality now. But what I see—what everyone in his life sees—is a very real spirituality. The man is transformed and continues to be transformed, the more he surrenders to that internal "still soft voice" he now knows he can rely on for reassurance and direction.

IF NOT FOR ME, WHO?

Unfortunately, not everyone is able to sustain this humble stance of "surrender." Sometimes, when not enough of a spiritual foundation has been laid, someone who becomes more materially successful as a result of making initial contact with his or her guardian angels' guidance screeches to a dead halt—and can start to spiral back into self-destruction. Some people who begin to enjoy success do not truly trust that it proceeds from an infinitely abundant universe. Often still operating from the secret conviction that they do not deserve success, they keep themselves from seeking the contact they need—daily, moment by moment—with the spiritual source of this abundance, and thus they eventually turn off its "tap." They begin to think that the "success" they've attained is the result of their own egoism and private machinations, and because secretly they don't feel deserving—indeed, they feel like impostors—the whole edifice often crumbles. Our angels want us to have abundance because it is the natural order of the Universe, but our own wounded egos often won't accept this fact.

This was the case with a former attorney I worked with as an actors' manager: as our business grew more successful, he became secretly more self-doubting and self-hating and turned to alcohol and drugs to escape his feelings of worthlessness. Because he did not trust the source of the abundance that had come so readily to him, it was as if he had to destroy it. When we're lucky, the collapse of our ego-built edifices can ram us into the realization that we must have a spiritual foundation for success. Our angels are joyful when we come to this realization because it means that now we can develop a truer self-love, an acceptance of our own worthiness, and once again participate in the natural abundance that is ours to have—and give.

The notion of "giving" is crucial. One actress who came to me was once part of a very successful and long-running television series and had, since the series had ended, descended into a bad funk. She hadn't been able to resuscitate her career—none of the roles she was offered gave her anything like the high-profile success she had previously enjoyed. She had gained weight, lost interest in her career, felt listless around her family, and generally fell into a deep depression. She came to me because she felt directionless—and she had heard from friends that I might be able to help her "jump start" her life back into gear.

As I explained in the first chapter, the experience of "plugging into" a client's energy is very much like turning on a radio and turning the dial until I pick up the "voices" of the angels who are always with that client. Of course, not only "voices" come to me—information can come in pictures or feelings or colors: our angels communicate with us in whatever way seems appropriate to the task at hand. But with this actress, whom I'll call Sandra, I got nothing but a kind of white noise static. Her depression was fogging up the airwaves. All Sandra had said before we started was "I just feel kind of lost." And indeed it was as if a light had been extinguished in her mind and heart: she had given up. Then I got a very strong message: Sandra needed to break a pattern. And the way for her to do that was, once again, to give herself permission to be who she was. Not the famous actress she had been a number of years ago. Not the "failure" she felt now by contrast to that past fame. Not the inadequate mother or wife she also felt she was. These self-lacerations were part of a droning pattern she had created out of her attachment to some old idea of who she thought she was supposed to be.

What finally came to me was the message that Sandra had to give to others right now. That she had to look for jobs that, whether or not they involved acting, *connected* her with people in a loving and giving way. She had to escape the prison she had constructed for herself. But first she had to make contact with who she really was—and this meant seeking contact with the source of who she was. I remembered when she first came to see me, I asked her why she had come. She'd said, "Well, for me. I mean, if this isn't for me, who is it for?"

She had labeled the problem neatly, I now realized. The help she sought wasn't for her—it was to help her connect with the source of who she was. It was to connect with God.

TAB: TAKE ACTION BEING

"Quiet down, make the connection, ask for help, take action, and let it go." In a few words, this is all you have to do to seek the connection Sandra needs and deeply wants to make. It describes a very different way to seek guidance from what most of us are taught. Surrender is at the heart of the process—letting go of your fears, offering them up to your angels, then asking, as simply as possible, for help. But doesn't this sound too easy? How could this bunch of nice-sounding New Agey words have much impact? Shouldn't I be giving you more elaborate instructions about how to "meditate"? Visualization exercises, Buddhist chants, Kabbalistic wisdom?

Actually, you *will* find a few specific "access your angel" suggestions at the end of the book. But whatever induces a meditative state in you is as individual as you are; ultimately only you can discover the particular path you need to follow to align your quest for angelic guidance with your temperament. You'll never be left stranded—even the barest first contact with an angel will allow that angel to help you deepen the connection. But you do have to make the first move in a way that's right for you.

Just remember: the simpler, the better. It's amazing how hungry our souls are for simple advice—how readily that businessman I talked about now acts "as if" his angels are right beside him (which of course they are!). There are no difficult algebraic equations to figure out here: all you need to do is surrender control for a moment—"quiet down"—so that you can "make the connection." You can depend upon your own hunger for this connection to guide you. Your angels *want* you to contact them: it is in all your interests that your means of "hearing" them or feeling their influence be as simple as possible. Don't expect this to be hard: it's not. Don't look for spirits and auras and ghosts as you look for your angels: just return to childhood and "pretend" that they're there. That's enough to beckon them closer to you. That's enough to open your soul's door to the guidance and unconditional love they offer you every moment of your life. Open the channels as simply as you can, and the infinite abundance of the universe will flood through.

But remember that receiving this gift of knowing what to do is not enough. The challenge is to take the action that this guidance makes clear. Generative actions don't come from our egos. They arise from *being*. Give yourself permission to *be*, give yourself permission to have your wildest and most wonderful dreams, give yourself permission to have all that your angels—and God—want you to have. When you do this, the action you first need to take to bring this abundance into being will suggest itself.

The acronym TAB—Take Action Being—is my shorthand for this process, to remind us to keep the horse before the cart. First just "be," then "make the connection" with your angels without worrying about or attempting to analyze who and what they are. "Ask for help," which if you've given yourself permission to "be" and have really "made the connection," I promise you will receive. Then "take the action" the help you receive will suggest. The outcome is assured: you needn't worry about it. Remember all that UN ambassador had to do was open the door and invite his guests in. Take the action of opening the door, and the rest of the great abundance your life deserves to be will flood in afterward.

Now that we know generally what it means—and how essentially simple it is—to receive the guidance from our guardian angels that is so infinitely available to us, let's turn our attention more specifically back to the angels who give it. As much as your perception of your guardian angels may wane and wax—some of my clients have quite clear ideas of who their angels are, as I have a clear idea of mine; others continue happily "as if" and enjoy the same benefits of guidance—there are certain groups of angels to whom you can appeal when your own inner promptings urge you, as Sandra's angels were urging her, to "break a pattern." These "types" of angels can help you to create a vision of the life you want, increase wisdom, understand and appreciate purity of thought and motive, cultivate true inner strength, enhance your sense of love and peace, and allow yourself to participate joyously in the victory of living the life your angels urge you to live.

In other words, we are blessed with our own specific guardian angels, but we can also appeal to others for "special" help. It's as simple to make this exploration as it is to "quiet down" and make contact with the guardian angels you are already coming to know. Don't resist. Just come with me and find out more about the infinite sources of help to which you have always had and always will have access. If you get stuck or find yourself disbelieving, permit yourself to pause for a moment, "quiet down," reactivate the curiosity, courage, and imagination you had as a child—and act "as if." That's all you need to do to keep the door to your angels wide open.

3
THE ANGEL OF VISION

The seven angels we will investigate in this and the next six chapters offer very specific guidance. Each has a particular and separate focus. But as distinct as each of these angels is, each—from Vision to Victory—connects intimately to every other. And their order is not an accident.

I learned this some years ago, when a very wise teacher and guide suggested that I meditate on and seek guidance from seven angels, *in the order* in which she then itemized them:

The Angel of Vision
The Angel of Wisdom
The Angel of Purity
The Angel of Strength
The Angel of Love
The Angel of Peace
The Angel of Victory

While I had questions about the nature of these angels, I knew that these questions would be answered if I just followed her instructions: meditate, and allow each angel to "speak" to me. I trusted my teacher, who had never told me more or less, at any given moment, than I needed to know. And she knew that now it was enough just to list the realms with which these angels were associated. Their importance would be revealed to me if I simply meditated on each, one after the other.

I already had intuitions about the angels' chronology just by looking at the list. But I would truly learn why they were listed in this order only by embracing each of them in turn—asking for each's particular guidance. I would learn about the importance of their chronology—and help my clients to learn it—first by experiencing in my own life the lessons and gifts of each angel and the link each had to the next one in the progression. This didn't mean I couldn't appeal to one angel "out of sequence." We often find ourselves doing that. But I learned that if I hadn't laid the spiritual foundation to make full use of a particular angel's help—a foundation that the preceding angels would have helped me to create—I wouldn't be able completely to enjoy the benefits of the angel to whom I'd turned.

IS THERE AN ANGELIC ETIQUETTE?

Sometimes when I talk about these angels, people wonder how any one of them could possibly guide every human being who seeks their particular guidance. Surely there are many angels of vision, many of wisdom, and so on? Other clients wonder what these angels have to do with the special angel guides we also always have. Is there an angelic etiquette to follow here—one angel we should consult before another? Do they all get together to "discuss our cases" as if in a board meeting? Who's the head honcho?

My answer is practical. Don't worry about it. Just ask the angel or angels in question for help. Open your heart to their guidance, and it will come. Knowing that it *will* come is one of the best ways to prove the truth of this. It's not that cosmological questions aren't interesting. From time to time I'll offer various reflections and observations that have come to me through my own angels and spiritual guides about the nature of the spiritual realms they inhabit and to which we have continual and infinite access. But strange as it may sound, these "big" questions are not crucial. Far more important is to ask for—and make abundant *use* of—these angels' loving help. As I've suggested, you don't even have to believe in angels to receive their help. It is enough to *act as if* each angel is there for you and you alone. All you have to do is ask. They want to help you—they are helping you already. As always, all you have to do is open your heart to them to find this out.

This also is the most helpful answer I know to give to anyone who is anxious to know the identity of his or her guardian angel(s). Remember that my guardian angel chose when to reveal himself to me: the Archangel Michael came exactly at the point when I was most receptive to him, when I would be most helped by "seeing" and becoming conscious of him. Trust that if a similar revelation happens to you now or later (or even not at all), you're being treated in the best possible way for you. Your angels take care of you perfectly. Ask for their guidance, and you will receive it: ask to "see" or know more about the specific angelic source of that guidance, and you may— depending on what your angel(s) determine is best for you—detect a sweet scent that reminds you of someone you loved as a child, hear a faint haunting phrase or song lyric that precisely soothes some deep ache in you, or see the glimmer of a face with an expression of such caring and warmth that your heart is set immediately at ease. You may also witness the emergence of a whole "being" who introduces him- or herself by name. (That may be the last time you have such a vision. I have only seen the Archangel Michael once, at the moment he revealed himself to me in Notre Dame. But he is no less real to me now than he was then.) The point is: you are being embraced and guided no matter what angelic manifestation you are enabled to see, feel, smell, hear, or otherwise register in your mind and senses. Angels don't depend for their existence on our conscious perception of them.

Just trust in that. And then let them do the job of guiding you that they so joyfully and eagerly want to carry out.

YOU CAN'T HAVE ONE WITHOUT THE OTHER

For your optimal happiness and satisfaction, you are well advised to open your heart to *all* of the angels you will read about here—and heed their guidance. The full range of benefits they offer is important, not just to help you acquire the goal you've set for yourself but to strengthen your capacity to sustain and cultivate your enjoyment of having reached that goal. You can't have one angel without the other. Well, you can—indeed, we'll meet a couple of people who've attempted this—but you'll find that if you concentrate on the prospect of only one angel's gifts, eventually you will stumble over an unanticipated bump farther down the road—a "bump" that another angel's guidance would have helped you to avoid.

Sometimes even people who have enjoyed abundant help and

achieved striking material success from all seven angels will still, in a dark moment, lose faith, clench, shut down, become convinced that the sources of the "miraculous" help they've received have dried up. You may be blessed with sudden material success—more money, the job you've always longed for. You don't want to lose what you've gained, and you become afraid that you will lose it. Surely, you think, it was all a matter of chance or luck that you can't rely on to happen again. Or surely it happened only because of your own white-knuckled exertions. It didn't come because of any hocus-pocus spiritual or "angelic" help—what had ever made you believe that?

The real deal? If we don't tighten our grip, we'll lose what we have.

But we learn that this is the *un*real deal very soon.

One of my clients illustrates. Bill wanted to open a restaurant, but he had no confidence in his ability to negotiate with the financial backers, contractors, and suppliers he'd need. He came to me because no other source of advice (assertiveness training, cognitive therapy, and the like) had worked for him, helped him to overcome his fear. Spiritual help was his last resort.

I helped him to ask for the guidance he needed, to believe it was his already. He appealed (although at first without realizing it) to the Angel of Strength. He asked for the fortitude to carry out his intricate business plan. He asked for the "strength" to carry it through, not to give up while he bargained with a wide variety of people who he had been told were difficult.

The strength he'd asked for came to him: he enjoyed an amazingly smooth and stress-free passage from idea to opening day. Many of the contractors and suppliers he had expected to fear became his friends. Later, when he learned about the seven angels, he was quite clear that the Angel of Strength had helped him. What other angel could have given him such abundant power to "see it through"?

Later his old fears and assumptions began to return, however, and he started to doubt the source of the help he'd received. He soon became convinced that his success was all his own doing. Surely it was just by exerting his own willpower that he had somehow managed to get his restaurant going. Because he had not connected with the guidance offered by the angels preceding the Angel of Strength, he hadn't built a solid enough context or foundation for his success to continue and flourish. Before long, he began to shut down—became his old, nervous, mistrustful self. He became suspicious of his suppliers, who then stopped giving him the attention and price breaks they had freely offered before. His once-successful restaurant began to suffer because of his "control freak" decisions and actions.

Angels tell us that help is infinitely abundant and available, and that we always have more guidance than we know. But these gifts and guidance are not bestowed once and for all. To sustain them and prosper, we must remain receptive—willing to grow and change. Our spiritual growth and material success flourish only when we recognize that they are *ongoing*. Only when we embrace the flow of our angels' help, and respond to it openly, with all our hearts, can it expand. But the best (really the only) way to learn this is to undergo the whole progression of guidance that the seven angels offer us.

And we need it—all of it. Like Bill, most of us experience moments of fearing that we can't make the leap our angels encourage us to make. Most of us feel at times that if we don't tighten our grip, we'll lose everything. It is human to be afraid of change, to be afraid to take the risks our angels encourage us to take, tell us we need to take. Luckily, these angels help us through our resistance not only by conferring the blessings of their own particular gifts but also by preparing us for the next angel to come. Which, with their help, I hope also to do here.

WHY THE ANGEL OF VISION IS FIRST

Bill certainly had a picture of the restaurant he wanted to open, but he did not have a vision of it. The Angel of Vision offers much more than the opportunity to "picture" in a tunnel-vision way the particular outcome you feel you need or want. Vision is deeper than sight, even imaginative sight. And maybe most important to remember: vision is a *gift*. The information that true vision gives you is invaluable—it enables you to see not only the life you truly want but your own complicity in the life you have right now. It allows you to take inventory of your habits and patterns.

So the first thing to remember about this all-important preliminary step is simply this: ask for the gift of vision from this angel. Ask this angel for everything you need to know to reach the goal or achieve the life you want.

Sometimes the goal you start out thinking you want will, with the gift of vision, reveal itself as inadequate—not big enough, not complete enough. Vision can give you the information you need to find your "calling" in life. One of my clients, Andrea, learned this very quickly when she was able to let go and truly ask the Angel of Vision for help. In her late thirties, the single divorced mother of two junior-high-aged kids, Andrea came to me just having lost her job and having no idea how to meet her bills—especially her mortgage payments. She was sure she'd be out on the street, and she had no idea how to stop what she felt as a tidal pull to complete disaster. She had completely shut down with fear. "I don't know how to do it!" had become her negative mantra: she felt completely powerless to improve anything in her life.

I asked her to remember when she was a little girl and played pretend. Or to think of her own kids when they were little and they imagined a whole magical world that they then played in. She was able to escape to this state of childlike wonder fairly easily—its freedom was so preferable to the imminent catastrophe she felt "real life" held for her. Her face softened, she smiled, as she allowed herself to go back to being that little girl. "Now," I said, "you have the perfect job that pays all your bills and will allow you to do what you love." I asked her to repeat that, saying "I." She did.

I asked her to call upon the Angel of Vision to help her. I got from my own angels a clear picture of a temp job at a movie studio that she would be offered. I knew that it could be the beginning of something, could lead her to the sort of job she wanted. She revealed to me that she'd always wanted to be a screenwriter. I told her, when she was offered the job, to take it. But first, to act as if she already had the perfect job—and to ask for guidance, for the vision to see everything about this perfect life as clearly as she could.

She was offered the job I'd foreseen within the week. At first she complained, "But it's only part time! I wanted a full-time job." I told her to embrace it anyway, that it would lead to something greater. A secretarial job in the publicity department, Andrea's position also required her to write—which, when she submitted her first assignments, caught the eye of her boss. "You're really good," her boss told her. The three-day-a-week job turned full time within two weeks. Already she was able to make her mortgage payments.

"But I want to write a screenplay!" she told me at a subsequent session. I told her once again to ask for the vision of what this would entail—a vision of the screenplay and the life that she would be leading while writing it "as if" it were already happening. "It *is* happening now—that's how I want you think of it, that's what I want you to see." And the Angel of Vision allowed her to experience this life "as if" it were happening, to give her the experience of living the life *now* that she thought she'd never be able to achieve. The Angel of Vision tells us to act as if the "picture" we see is already perfect and already here.

The next day Andrea's boss asked her to take home a book that a friend of his had written and to write a screen treatment of it. He thought he might be able to interest the studio in turning it into a movie, and that Andrea was a natural to be the screenwriter.

Abundance continues to flow to Andrea, as long as she'll receive it. But it's what she's learned from the experience of accepting this abundance that's important. As you can see, when the dominoes began to fall in her favor—the job appeared, changed from part time to full time, involved writing, led to her boss recognizing her talent, which led to the possibility of writing a screenplay—at every new, exciting, and promising juncture, Andrea's first response was to freeze and say, "But!" "But it's not full time, but I want to write a screenplay," and so on.

The Angel of Vision finally not only gave Andrea the picture of what she wanted and allowed her to see how achievable this picture was, but more subtly this angel allowed Andrea to confront her

"But!"s—to see that her own resistance to change, even positive change, was the potential problem. The Angel of Vision in some ways automatically holds up a mirror so that we can see not only how effortlessly abundance can flow to us, but that the only thing impeding that flow is our own fear, our own belief somehow that we do not deserve the abundance that "wants" to come to us.

THE PROBLEM ISN'T GETTING WHAT YOU WANT—IT'S ACCEPTING IT WHEN IT COMES!

Andrea's story goes on—she's working on the screen treatment as of this writing. But the abundance didn't stop there. As a lark, she applied to be a contestant on a TV game show, was accepted, and won $30,000. "I didn't even ask for that!" she said delightedly, but somewhat dazed. Then almost too unbelievably (to Andrea), she struck up a conversation with a handsome man who worked on the TV show, the chemistry was unmistakable, and she's now dating him. But she's scared, she tells me. "I'm not used to stuff going right all the time. I feel like I have to pull down the shades and hide for a while. Surely this can't continue!"

She began to see, with her Angel of Vision's help, that while material success and pleasure are infinitely available, they have to "fall" on fertile ground truly to take root: like rain on soil rich enough to sustain the fruit and foliage that grow from it. She saw that she had to love herself before she could feel deserving, before she could feel she was allowed to have all this abundance.

The Angel of Vision throws this important lesson into sharp relief for us. Alas, for some people the fears and self-mistrust are so great that they continue to be blind to this lesson—with sometimes very unfortunate consequences.

Jack, 35, who moved from a farm town in Nebraska to Los Angeles about ten years ago, says he always felt like a "hick." "I feel I have to compensate for all the stuff I didn't learn, growing up with cows and chickens instead of people." So he put himself on a regimen of reading whole libraries of books, took himself to Europe for "civilization," became an expert on Ibsen and Strindberg, and returned to the United States determined to make his mark in the higher end of the "entertainment industry." "I wanted to do the casting for Merchant Ivory or something," he says. "I imagined all sorts of wonderful lunches with Daniel Day-Lewis and Emma Thompson."

What Jack did manage to do was get a low-level agency job where he handled C-list clients who were considerably less impressive than the high-class quarry he was after. He came to me when he felt as if he'd never get off the bottom rung.

I knew Jack needed the Angel of Vision's help—again, not just to see the job and life he wanted, and to act as if they already were his, but to see his own feelings of self-worthlessness, which were what my own angels were telling me really had stopped him cold. He eagerly meditated with me and described in great detail the business he knew he could do if only he had his own agency. I told him I saw a partner who would be willing to back him, if he just worked out a business plan and an eloquent "statement of intent." This vision took root immediately in his mind—and once again, within two weeks of this session, Jack was introduced at a party to a wealthy patron of the arts who was looking to become involved in precisely the kind of agency Jack wanted to create.

As with Bill, Jack's success was immediate and startling. He made field trips to the Yale School of Drama and Juilliard and Northwestern and the Actors Studio, often acquiring the crème-de-la-crème of their graduates and giving them the first boost they needed. Very quickly, his agency got an industrywide rep as "a class act." Money began to pour in, and prestige.

And with the money and prestige came a great deal of cocaine. The "entertainment industry" is notoriously drug laden, and Jack was an addict waiting to happen. He began taking expensive trips, over-spending not only on cocaine but on a fancy impressive BMW and an apartment he could not afford and—well, you get the picture. The whole edifice of his successful life became top-heavy, and it was only a matter of time before it collapsed on his head.

Jack makes me sigh deeply—as he probably makes you sigh, per-haps in identification with him, perhaps because you know others like him whose own self-hatred (largely hidden to them) continually sabotages them. The Angel of Vision offers so much more than a pic-ture of success. It was Jack's unwillingness to seeing this "more"—to seeing the full picture of himself as well as of the life he yearned for—that eventually caused the collapse.

Once again, we need a spiritual foundation for success to sustain itself. The Angel of Vision gives you the first groundwork for this all-important foundation. You need not only to ask for this angel's help but also to receive it. All of it. Which will necessarily entail receiving a vision of who you are, and what it may be advisable for you to look at—and change—so that you can do what this and all the other angels want you to do: thrive.

MAKING SURE THE VISION UNDERNEATH IS WHAT YOU WANT

We always manifest exactly what we want. This may sound like lunacy to you: "But I don't want to be broke, or in this awful job, or in the terrible relationship I'm in! How can you say that?"

I'm not the only one who says it: so does the Angel of Vision. The full array of your life that the Angel of Vision wants you to see isn't just the "prize" dangling like a carrot in front of your nose: as I've suggested, it's also the full impact of your past and present on your life. Indeed, to make the Angel of Vision's essential gift "work," you do need to see the life you want as "already here." But you also need to be compassionate toward yourself about the wounds of your past, your childhood. Jack didn't talk about it with me at first, but he later told me that his father was an alcoholic—"an alcoholic farmer," Jack said, "which means he made his own corn liquor and basically allowed the farm to go bust"—and Jack was regularly beaten as a little boy for no more reason than that the father thought it would "toughen him up."

These wounds need healing. These angels will help you to heal them. But no healing is possible without the willingness to see the wound—not to wallow in it, not to base the vision of your life on it, but to acknowledge its existence. If you don't, its impact can be relied upon to sabotage the works: witness Bill (who had his own childhood "stuff" he wasn't looking at); witness Jack.

Already with this first angel in the progression, we learn something essential: yes, the Angel of Vision wants your life to be a feast, wants you to envision that feast in enough specificity, and with enough attention to your real desires, that you will know how to manifest it. But each angel's function (as we'll see again and again) is not only to bestow the miracle of that angel's particular gift but also to "heal" you so that your experience of joy will not be impeded by early wounds, especially the wounds you may have blocked out from consciousness, buried out of remembrance. My experience of the Angel of Vision always has this quality of preparing me for the next stage: I'm enabled to "see" the vision and am simultaneously invited to surrender to whatever it is that I must understand or do in order to make that vision reality. This always has a somewhat disturbing initial effect, because we're always asked to *trust* absolutely in the guidance we're offered—trust that we need to take the leap our angels tell us the next stage of growth requires of us. Even after my guardian angel, the Archangel Michael, revealed himself to me—and reassured me I didn't have to have the material concerns I had (no money and no place to live in Paris)—I experienced the odd panicked moment, until I was able once again to make contact with the gift of Michael's presence, enough to help me, at once, to let go of the noisy fearful arguments in my head.

Healing is the great angelic goal, even if the aim starts out to be something quite different. The joyful news is that we can get the prize we seek and be healed. Indeed, the prize and the healing are interconnected: we can't truly have or enjoy one without the other.

Consider Marie. So much in her professional life quickly and dramatically fell into place, and yet something was buried inside her, something against which she had protected herself so completely for so long that no conscious memory of it remained. But like the proverbial pea under the mattress, this uncomfortable "spot" in her psyche eventually made itself known. The clearer she got in other areas of her life, the more any impediment or distorted perception was laid bare. As you'll see, her angels were ready to help her face this internalized block and let it go.

Marie is French and came to this country with her American husband. Just about from the moment they landed on these shores, he became abusive—nothing like the man she'd thought she'd married. "I didn't know what to do. I spoke enough English to get along. We already had a little daughter. I knew I couldn't live with him—we had to divorce. And he didn't seem to care at all about what happened to me or his child. He even suggested that Jackie wasn't his."

Marie came to me with very little hope—someone, a casual friend, had suggested that she might need a "spiritual" reading and had recommended me, and she decided to give it a try. When I helped her to clear her mind and begin to meditate, I very quickly got the picture of a salon in Beverly Hills and Marie as its proprietress. I told her about the vision, and she laughed. "Well, I came here hoping to start an aromatherapy business, but I never thought of it as a Beverly Hills operation! Surely it is too New Age for that!" But now that the vision was articulated—and once she accepted it—it took root.

The short version of this story is that she began to import flower essences from France and sell them at first from her home and then from—you guessed it—a boutique in Beverly Hills. Like Jack and Bill and Andrea, she began almost immediately to partake of abundance—of precisely the "success" she never thought was possible.

But what also began to manifest in her life was a series of men who were just as abusive as the husband Marie had divorced. "Why does this keep happening?" she said to me. And I asked her to ask for the guidance and help that might clarify why it was happening. Again: we needed the Angel of Vision's help. In a guided meditation, Marie began to describe a picture in her head: "It's my mother, crying...I hear voices in the house, yelling, and I hear my mother shouting back, 'No! No! I won't go back in!' There is obviously a terrible fight inside. I can't make out who it is—" And then Marie stopped for a moment. Tears began to collect and fall from her eyes. "It's me," she finally said. "My father—my father—" She couldn't complete the sentence.

Marie had remembered something she had blocked out for most of her adult life—a brief period ("It didn't last longer than my twelfth year") when, because her father had lost his job and the family had no money, his temper became horrendously volatile and he literally lashed out at the family. "My father had never beaten me before, and he never did after. It was like this terrible aberration—that vanished, thank God, almost as soon as it appeared. He was a loving man all through every other part of my childhood. It was this horrible year when he lost control—I never thought it was important, because it didn't last for long. But I guess..."

Having identified this wound and its source was ultimately tremendously healing to Marie. But the healing could not happen without help. She needed her angels' help and guidance. And she needed to know that this guidance is infinite—and would lead her finally to people who were truly nurturing, people whom she could really love and by whom she could be loved. She needed help—no less than the rest of us—from the next angel in the progression, the Angel of Wisdom.

4
THE ANGEL OF WISDOM

You know now that the Angel of Vision offers so much more than a picture of whatever life you may have dreamed of, prayed for, or yearned for. You know from "entering" the vision that it isn't some pipe dream. In some ways, it's already a reality—a kind of imminent reality brought on by the vividness of imagining it, and the Angel of Vision's powerful reassurance that it's yours if you want it. The Angel of Vision *wants* what *you* want to manifest. One of the most wondrous aspects of this angel's encouragement is that it enables you to imagine having the life you want *right now*—to act "as if" it were here already. In some ways (having created it in your mind), it *is* here already. The Angel of Vision gives you certainty not only that this vision is achievable but that envisioning it is the first step toward giving it actual form.

But you need the help of another angel before you can get this process of manifestation going, another angel eager to help with focus and logistics (as well as some deeper purposes). That angel is already at your side—in fact, is helping you already: the Angel of Wisdom.

This angel offers crucial help, ultimately pragmatic help, as you're guided to "right" actions, without which no one can manifest anything. (Having a vision without taking action to make it reality amounts to wishful thinking.) So a crucial part of the "wisdom" this angel offers is to help you discover what you'll need to make your particular "miracle" happen.

But what if you're still not clear about your goal?

As essential as an overall vision is, making any part of it reality must be driven by a precise and heartfelt "motive": what I call "intention." The Angel of Wisdom helps you to identify and embrace this all-important basic: *intention.*

Nothing worthwhile can be created without energy and focus, but intention is more than either of these. Intention is as passionate and caring as it is particular and directive: it's the personal and emotional investment you make in both the process and the outcome of bringing your "vision" to life. And when you consciously engage angels in this kind of heartfelt intention, asking for their help and support (particularly from the Angel of Wisdom, who helped you first find and open your creative power), amazing things are guaranteed to happen; you will be helped in unexpected ways by unforeseen sources. Surprise visits from long unseen friends, long-distance phone calls, (seemingly) chance encounters, sudden travel opportunities, introductions to people you've always wanted to meet, financial and/or creative windfalls, all kinds of (seeming) serendipity: these are only a few examples of the kind of "responses" a clear passionate intention will (with the Angel of Wisdom's help) call up. Boons and go-aheads and gifts abound.

Another miracle's always waiting to happen.

THE LARGER PURPOSE: KARMIC PART OF WISDOM

Clarity, the clarity of intention, of identifying specifically what you want; the intensity of caring deeply about achieving the outcome; and then, with the Angel of Wisdom's guidance, taking the "right actions" that serve the intention—these are the basics of pursuing and manifesting a vision. The Angel of Wisdom asks us to help the process along in another way, however: to *know* (and reaffirm) that the vision wants to manifest. Even more, to know (and reaffirm) that it *should* manifest.

Suggesting that a sought-after vision "should" manifest connects to another aspect of this angel's wisdom: karma. There are many different views of karma, but here's a simple definition: karma is life experience. It's the "stuff" of life that we're stuck with—the consequences of actions taken in past as well as current lives that have created spiritual imbalance. Angels (the Angel of Wisdom in particular) can guide us back to balance, can help us find ways to "pay back" or "give way" in some areas, and to take or even indulge ourselves in others: all corrective measures to reverse past misguided decisions and actions, particularly in past lives.

Don't worry if you don't believe in past lives or karma; as with other questions about cosmology, for the moment they don't really matter—the guidance you receive from angels will help you abundantly no matter what you believe about how the Universe works! Whether you see angelic guidance as an opportunity to change a bad habit or negative attitude, or whether you see it as repayment of a "karmic debt," you're going to be helped by it. That's all that matters.

The guidance offered by the Angel of Wisdom—because of the

many levels of suggestion this angel wants to impart—often seems to come to us in stages. These stages are always necessary, instructive, and loving, even if they may sometimes be frustrating in the short term or even inexplicable at first. But these are often experiences we must go through before we can identify the real "vision" of life we want for ourselves (not the vision we may think we're supposed to want)—rather like apprenticeships that we need to complete on the way to a larger, more satisfying goal.

The Angel of Wisdom teaches us that nothing happens without a reason—no guidance from any angel is unconsidered. We are always given what we need; we are never given more than we can handle. You've seen this in my own story. It began with the vision and experience of angels in Paris in Notre Dame—and at first I thought my destiny was to stay in France. But I was eventually brought back to Los Angeles, where I understood my work had to be centered. Only as I was able to register more and more information from spiritual guides, teachers, and angels did my real work of counseling reveal itself: counseling with the angels' help. Facing each stage of this journey felt like being called upon to make dangerous leaps. But the Angel of Wisdom has never let me down, then or now. And one of this angel's lessons has come from the revelation of some very powerful karmic pulls—to certain people, to France, to the work I'm now doing, and so on. The more I deliver myself to the guidance of the Angel of Wisdom, the more these karmic connections seem almost effortlessly to resolve—sometimes evolving into new, unforeseen friendships and opportunities.

A SECRET DESIGN

Darya's experience of the Angels of Vision and Wisdom was at first very private. A real estate agent who through the past decade or so became more and more disenchanted with her job, Darya especially hated being valued only as much as that particular month's number of sales and rentals. She said sometimes when she just couldn't stand the pressure of her boss breathing down her neck, "I'd get up from my desk on the pretext that I had to meet a client, and get in my car and drive to the ocean," she says. "Sometimes I'd just sit in my car and cry."

On one of these stolen trips to the shore, as she looked out over the ocean, something she had been "sitting on" finally surfaced in her mind. "There was something about the full unbroken expanse of the water in front of me," Darya said. "The colors, the sweep of sand and ocean—I knew what I wanted to do with my life, and it sure wasn't selling real estate." Darya had been "tinkering," as she put it, in her own home—trying out various design possibilities, new colors, different layouts of furniture. "I was working with a whole kind of 'sea palette.' Looking at the ocean somehow filled me with the confidence I needed really to make a go as a designer, using my own home as an experiment. I was determined to turn my home into a showcase— with a view to starting my own interior design business."

When I told her about the angels, Darya had no doubt that, on that last trip to the ocean, her barely articulated wish had been answered by the Angel of Vision. In that moment, she was given the gift of seeing her whole life as a designer. Her reputation quickly drew the kind of clients she wanted, clients who trusted her and would give her close to carte blanche to do what she wanted. Her life was filled with the creativity and the creative people she yearned for and had never experienced professionally before, certainly not as a real estate agent. The vision of her new life was overwhelming and brought tears of joy to her eyes.

"But those tears began to sting as I wondered how on earth I was going to shift gears from real estate to interior design at the age of 45, with no formal design background, very little time and money. I became as demoralized as I'd been hopeful. I knew I'd have to some-how do it while I worked—I couldn't afford to give up my real estate job while I pursed the design thing. But somehow my hope wasn't entirely stamped out. 'There must be a way,' I kept telling myself. Only later did I realize I was calling out for help—and the Angel of Wisdom answered."

It occurred to Darya to make up business cards. "I had a sudden vision of how I wanted them to look. I felt foolish—I hadn't com-pleted the design work on my house: how was I going to convince anyone I could do what I knew I could? But the certainty that I needed cards was stronger than any reservations I had. I also had some beautiful stationery made up: I was a business in letterhead and stationery before I was a business in real life!"

But this soon changed. She continued to work on her own home, and "Somehow I really was inspired. I like to think the Angel of Wisdom was by my side, passing on suggestions from the Angel of Vision." Her self-confidence grew. She knew she was creating the kind of showcase that really would attract clients. Then an associate at the real estate agency revealed that he had just bought twenty-four tract homes and was looking for a designer to spruce them up to increase their value. "I'm a designer," she said. "Come and see the interior I've just done." Darya evidently wowed this gentleman with the colors and low-cost approach she'd employed in her own home. He eagerly hired her. "One minute I had never done any work as a designer, the next I was designing twenty-four homes," Darya laughs quietly.

She's now happily severed relations with the real estate company, at least in her old capacity as agent. "Well, not completely severed," she says. "They were so impressed by what I did with the tract houses that they're recommending me to all sorts of clients—clients I was hoping to get. The life I'd seen for myself that day at the ocean is blossoming day after day, more wonderfully even than I'd envisioned."

The Angel of Wisdom helped Darya to work toward her vision first by dealing with her life as it was—to "keep her day job" while she designed and printed cards and stationery and turned her home into a showcase on weekends as evidence of her talent. Those twenty-four homes and various other jobs came from the agency she so disliked as an agent—but was able to see and use differently as a designer. Much of the "wisdom" of this angel encourages us to see the wealth of opportunity we've got under our noses. "I didn't realize what a gold mine that agency could be," Darya said. "Before this I hated my job so much that I couldn't see the agency as anything other than a prison. Now those doors have opened—and they look a lot more like gold than gunmetal."

STEP OUT OF YOUR COMFORT ZONE
(MOVE TOWARD TRUST)

I suggested before that of the many gifts the Angel of Wisdom would like us to embrace, one of the most important has to do with karma: the gift of achieving greater spiritual balance and alignment by taking certain "corrective" actions. This may sound awfully dreary, as if I'm backing away from my earlier assertion that angels are here to give you the pleasurable and exciting life you want, and am now suggesting that they're really out to dose you with spiritual castor oil, to get back at you for all the "bad" things you did in past lives you can't remember.

But the picture is not a grim one. "What's good for you" and what you love and yearn for in your life by no means exclude each other. The Angel of Wisdom can help you karmically to help yourself—at the same time you're being helped professionally and personally to achieve whatever vision you've longed for. The payoffs can be amazing: material wealth and success and a sense of spiritual satisfaction that you may never have known could be yours.

The catch? There isn't any—unless you regard having to trust, often with no apparent logical reason but with all your heart, as a catch. Certainly Mike had to be dragged kicking and screaming into the new notions that the Angel of Wisdom wanted him to embrace. At 28, Mike felt he was at a crossroads: he was an actor/singer who had done musicals and light comedy mostly in summer stock and dinner theater. "As a singer/actor on that circuit," he says, "I was very successful—really had nothing to complain about. I liked being an entertainer, I enjoyed the rapport I had with the audience. Well, most of the time. About a year ago, doing *The Fantastiks* for about the two hundred and sixty-fifth time in my life, I very nearly came to a halt. I somehow croaked through the performance, but when it was over, I felt like I had sung my last note. I was sick of being this chirpy dancing likable nobody. I knew I was capable of more depth, and I wanted to do drama—the big roles. I was pushing 30, after all; wasn't it time to do O'Neill? But once you get typecast as the kind of male soubrette I was…"

Mike felt considerable despair about changing midstream; he thought his agent would laugh him out of his office. "The guy had me on so many automatic lists, he barely had to do any work. I had about a half-dozen regular jobs and reliable contacts. But I felt like it was strangling me." This was when Mike came to me for help—and where he tenatively tried out the idea that angels could help him. "So I don't have to believe in them exactly?" he laughed at first. "Of course I *am* an actor—I guess I can convince myself…."

Mike already had a vision of the kind of actor he wanted to be— do more in films, including television films, maybe do a stint on a soap opera, which he knew could be a good if exasperating training ground. But his big fear was that everyone would laugh at him. "How could I possibly tell my agent? My parents? My friends? They're going to think I've turned into a John Malkovich wannabe—or worse." I asked him to ask for help from the Angel of Wisdom. I knew this angel offered much guidance from which Mike could benefit. "Just accept the gifts when they start to come," I told Mike. "Just say yes!" I knew that Mike's own negativity about his prospects could turn out to be his own worst stumbling block. "Just accept, keep smiling, open your arms—and get out of your own way."

Mike meditated on the Angel of Wisdom and asked for help. About two nights afterward, he told me, he fell asleep and dreamed a disturbing but very vivid dream. "It was odd. I could tell it was me in the dream, except I didn't look like myself at all. This guy was blond and sort of German looking—about as far from my dark Mediterranean looks as you could get. But I knew it was me. And I didn't like what he was doing. He was stealing from a store on the corner. Then I saw him at a party, where he grabbed at a woman and dragged her off to a closet—he was this amoral sensual beast of a kid. And he seemed like a kid—totally irresponsible, totally selfish—but maybe most disturbing because I could tell he was me. I woke up from the dream with the strongest resolve I'd ever had to make a change in my acting career." Mike laughed. "What was the connection between seeing this irresponsible kid in my dream and this new resolve? I can't believe I'm saying this, but it felt like it was karmically right to pursue a more serious dramatic career. I felt like I was looking at a past life—a life in which I had been completely superficial and hedonistic. My light little musicals were sort of keeping me that superficial kid."

Whether or not Mike had a karmic vision of himself isn't the point: what did ensue was a much more concerted appeal to the Angel of Wisdom to help him shift gears. One of the welcome effects of this strange dream was to rid Mike of any fear of revealing the change he wanted to make. He even called his agent, who—far from laughing at him—recommended an Actors Studio teaching group he thought would be great for Mike. He also said that Mike was visually perfect for a two-part television movie that was casting that week and that he hadn't thought of Mike only because he was convinced Mike wouldn't have been interested—it wasn't *The Fantastiks!* While auditioning for this role, he was approached by another actor who was sure he'd known Mike from sometime long past—it turned out the guy had been in one of the dinner-theater productions Mike had starred in a good ten years before. "I'd always hoped I'd meet you again," this guy said. "You were my role model back then. I hoped ever since to talk about the theater world with you—maybe even take lessons with you!"

Mike went through his share of "clench episodes," as he called them. "That Actors Studio scared the pants off me," he says. "I could barely speak. Everything I did came out wrong. The exercises just made me feel more awkward. What made me think I could be a serious actor?" Many times Mike decided he'd made a mistake—and stopped trusting in the help he'd unfailingly gotten from the Angel of Wisdom. But he held on—he kept remembering that dream, and what felt like the karmic necessity to live a more committed and fulfilling life as a man and as an artist. The TV movie gave him confidence: self-confidence that traveled over to the Actors Studio group. He amazed himself: he was gaining technique—and respect. He's now up for a major film role. "I've moved from thinking of myself as two-bit lounge lizard to—well, now my agent's calling me the next Kevin Spacey. Not that there needs to be one. But who'd have put me in the same sentence with him two years ago?"

With angelic help (Mike is convinced it was a dream induced by the Angel of Wisdom), Mike may have stumbled onto some karmic reasons for wanting to shift gears in his professional life to become more disciplined and accomplished as an actor, with more heartfelt "intention." Certainly that's what he's doing—and he is experiencing success in a theatrical realm that once seemed constitutionally beyond his reach. When karmic imbalances are righted, success can be instantaneous, almost as if, without knowing it, you and the people around you were yearning for balance to be restored. That's how Mike says it *feels,* no matter what the actual karmic "reality" may be.

The Angel of Wisdom's main role is primarily what we've identified: offering you the guidance and resources to begin to manifest your dreams—and teaching you in the course of this that it's simple! It's a matter of trusting and following guidance that you may hear most clearly as an inner voice or experience simply as a nonverbal urging.

But the Angel of Wisdom also helps you moment to moment, sometimes by alerting you to the misbehavior of others. The Angel of Wisdom can "clear the frequencies," to help you see and hear through the cover-ups and evasions of other people in your life. Many of my clients speak of getting sudden illuminations about colleagues or business partners who have cheated them or embezzled money: they credit the Angel of Wisdom as the source of these illuminations. Once again, karma is the point, not vengeance. To help someone or oneself avoid a karmic misdeed lightens the spirit and clears the way for the kind of successful and fulfilled lives we all deserve. But you can depend upon the Angel of Wisdom to keep you alert to the misdeeds of others as well as increase your own alertness across the board.

The Angel of Wisdom is similarly invaluable in relationships, once again helping to illuminate uncomfortable facts and secrets. One woman who'd been married for over twenty years had tried, she said, to ignore a sense of aloneness in her marriage, but she now had to acknowledge that her loneliness had grown to intolerable intensity.

She'd turned to alcohol and drugs to muffle the ache, now she had stopped losing herself in chemicals, had come to me for help, and found almost immediate solace from the Angel of Wisdom, who made it clear that she needed a time of living on her own to learn that she could depend upon her own resources to be fulfilled and happy. "It sounds like cliché women-out-to-find-themselves stuff," Anna says, "but the certainty and strength of this inner urging to live alone and to learn to trust myself—well, I could neither ignore nor dismiss it as some message from my own superego. It was unquestionably angelic!"

Engage the Angel of Wisdom as completely as you can, and you'll learn an invaluable lesson. With a powerful intention rooted in an authentic vision, a readiness to act energetically on that intention, and a heart open to every eventuality, you can create precisely the happy and particular life you want—a life that makes joyful use of all you are—and one, as Anna has learned, that is not neurotically dependent on the presence of anyone else.

But the Angel of Wisdom also teaches that "right actions" always have in them a measure of *being*, not just "doing." My experience swimming today is a more reliable meditative technique than it was when I swam competitively because I don't have the same nerve-wracking agenda I had when I'd hoped to make the Olympic team. Even then, as I've said, I would "tune out" every time I swam, but only later was I able to use it as a tool. Therefore, full of the revelation the Angel of Wisdom has given me, I now swim to achieve a state of being that I know will be helpful to me. This doesn't happen only when I swim. It's amazing the variety of opportunities we're offered to "take action being": going to the dentist is a transformative experience for

73

me. The second I hit the chair, I drift off to a meditative state that always brings me joy and peace, and sometimes some good ideas about whatever creative challenge I've been grappling with. Now I can't wait to go the dentist! Resourcefulness: this, resoundingly, is what the Angel of Wisdom teaches us we have in infinite measure.

And with this infinite resourcefulness, and with patience and love, the Angel of Wisdom awaits you now: to help you bring every last aspect of your "intention" to life.

5

THE ANGEL OF PURITY

Helping us like fraternal twins, the Angels of Vision and Wisdom simultaneously suggest both perspective and plan—guiding us to take whatever actions are necessary to satisfy our deepest yearnings, to bring our dreams to life. As we've seen, if we truly embrace the plans they offer us, if we trust enough to take the "leaps" they beckon us to take, the results can be miraculous. Witness the abrupt success in the lives of the several people we've already looked at—so abrupt sometimes that they were temporarily dazed by it, even while their perceptions changed forever about the bounty they now saw their angels wanted them to have in life. From Bill the restaurateur asking for and suddenly receiving the self-confidence to negotiate with suppliers and contractors; to Andrea who within weeks of being jobless suddenly found herself writing a screen treatment for a major studio, something she'd dreamed of doing all her life; to Darya making the transformation from overworked real estate drudge to spectacularly successful interior design artist; to Mike who made a leap into more dramatic roles as an actor and found himself almost instantly employed in theater and television, making more money and feeling greater satisfaction than he ever had: all these people learned to some degree to "get out of their own way" and trust the angels' messages they heard internally. They were then able to benefit immediately from all the gifts the Angels of Vision and Wisdom were so eager to bestow.

Offering the gift of a goal and a practicable plan for achieving it, teaching us that right actions are the real agents of change, that we can always rely on the Angel of Wisdom's guidance to pursue whatever the next "right action" may be, as well as to gain a deeper appreciation of the larger "karmic" purpose of the paths we want and are encouraged to take—these gifts are so powerful that it's natural to wonder: what more could we possibly want? Why would we need any further guidance from any other angel? These gifts already seem more bountiful than we ever dared imagine.

As much as I've suggested that the chronology of these seven angels is important, when you cast your eye over the rest of the angels in the progression—Purity, Strength, Love, Peace, and Victory—you may wonder about their relative importance. Do you really need all of them? And with the success you'll have had with the Angels of Vision and Wisdom, is it really all that important which angel you query next for help? Perhaps you can see the value of Strength arising where it does—maybe it's a sort of angelic pit-stop where you can refuel on stamina midjourney. And who wouldn't want to achieve the promised Victory? Isn't that the point of all this—to emerge victorious?

But you may wonder about the rest. For instance, why does Peace come before Victory? (Wouldn't it be nicer to settle into "peace" *after* "victory," like a tired warrior falling into a soft bed?) Come to think of it, why are *any* of the other angelic monikers—Purity, Love, and Peace—where they are? Shouldn't Love have come before all else?

Why is it wedged between Strength and Peace? Why does Purity pop up in between Wisdom and Strength?

The Angel of Purity, in particular, may strike you as problematic. "Purity" is awfully Puritan-sounding: is this a do-it-because-it's-good-for-you antidote to all the pleasure and fulfillment that all the other angels seem to be offering you without question? A kind of arbitrary moral cleanser we have to scrub ourselves with before we can get to more of the "good stuff"?

I said at the outset that when these angels were introduced to me, my teacher said their order was crucial—but that I would truly learn why only by meditating on each in turn. I'm teasing you a bit with the "chronology question" again to underscore this point: it is *your* grappling with, *your* meditation on each of these angels that will prove to you why they are in the order they're in. I'm confident you'll find that their order is profoundly important—and surprising. The meaning of these angels and the way they interact with each other is not, I believe I can guarantee, what you're expecting. As you'll see from your own embrace and investigation of them, the progression of angels amounts to a progression of steps, no one of which can profitably be taken in isolation or out of sequence. By now the Angels of Vision and Wisdom are somewhat self-explanatory in this regard: it makes sense that you have to "see" what you want to accomplish before you can take "wise" actions to make it a reality.

Although it may not seem as inevitably placed, the Angel of Purity awaits you right after the Angel of Wisdom for innumerable good reasons, none of them arbitrary, and none of them repressive or moralistic. Think of the Angel of Purity as a fresh exhilarating shower of cool water—a kind of spiritual palate cleanser—a joyful opportunity to reconnect to the clarity you were offered at the start by the Angel of Vision, but that you now find you are ready to take even deeper into your heart and soul. It's a call to stay as true as possible to the selfless, joyful pact you made with the Angels of Vision and Wisdom and yourself. Asking for help from this angel now is crucially timed (after the Angel of Wisdom and before the Angel of Strength). Without this angel's lucidity and direction, without the joyful and *selfless* purpose it floods us with like a sudden spring shower, we easily become prey to a very natural human egotism: we are likely to become suspicious that the source of the help we've received is more fluke than infinite flow (remember Bill the restaurateur, whose growing self-absorption and fearful wariness slowly strangled the success of his business?); to believe that whatever blessings we've enjoyed have come as the product of our own tight-fisted exertions and not from an eternal bounty.

The Angel of Purity allows us to keep the channels clear, just when we need them to be. Without this angel's cleansing power, our streams tend to become muddy with our own fears and egotism—and we'd drift away from the clarity and joy we're offered if we'd only continue to trust openly and selflessly in our angel's guidance. The Angel of Purity also reminds us how *simple* this whole process of asking for and receiving help is. All we ever need do is trust that guidance will come—and trust in it when it does come. All we ever need do is listen to the answers we receive and take the actions those answers imply. It is as if the Angel of Purity were singing out in the clear crystal notes of a rushing stream: *This is your route to joy! All you need to do is follow me!*

THE HIDDEN ARROGANCE OF DESPAIR

Outwardly because of pride, inwardly because of a hidden fear that we'll lose what we've gained if we don't "take back the reins," there is often—as we've seen—a kind of arrogance and egotism that arises in people who've enjoyed an upswing in fortune. It proceeds out of a growing mistrust that the "flow" will stop, or has stopped already, and that our only recourse is to hold on to what we've already got. Fear causes us to tighten and shrink, often leading to "control freak" tendencies that may sometimes look on the surface like strength or self-assertion but that in fact deaden growth, stop the flow. The Angel of Purity can save anyone who is in these desperate ego-ridden straits: as always, all you have to do is open your heart and ask for this angel's help to reconnect with the flow of abundance that wants to come to you.

Our need for the Angel of Purity is not always obvious. Sometimes, especially when we undergo painful or even tragic circumstances, we may experience a loss of faith—a different kind of clenching from the arrogant "I'm the source of my own good fortune" that can happen when we're afraid we'll lose what we've gained. We don't swing in the direction of arrogance at such times of despair; we swing quite radi-cally to its opposite: hopelessness. Rather than thinking we can wrest success out of the universe through sheer self-serving will (the most common fallacy that the Angel of Purity seeks to debunk), at moments of great despair we become convinced that there is no recourse left to us at all, and that we are destined to be buffeted by whatever fate decides to deliver. Even if we continue to give lip service to belief in a "higher power" that is somehow "in charge," the secret personal truth is that we've given up. The Angel of Purity can help such despairing people with sometimes inexpressible beauty and tenderness and clarity. Witness what happened to 82-year-old Virginia, once she was able to surface from her own despair and ask for this angel's help.

Virginia is a beautiful woman in her eighties—and she has quietly believed in and sought help from angels for many decades. "It's not something I tell a lot of people," she says. "I'm always afraid people will think I ought to be institutionalized if I go into too much detail about the communing I've done with angels." The prospect of being "institutionalized" is particularly and poignantly upsetting to Virginia because her husband, 87-year-old Herman, is in the late stages of Alzheimer's and has been in a combination hospital/nursing home for the past six months. "Until six months ago," Virginia says, "I was able to keep him home with the help of aides who'd come in the morning and in the evening to change him and take him out or put him back into bed." Her blue eyes grow wistful: "It was the last good time, really, we had. He could still be picked up and taken to a day care center, where they told me he hummed and sang and smiled and flirted with the nurses! I was so glad that he had some sort of life even while it was clear to me he didn't have a clue who I was any-more." But then Herman, in an attempt to get out of his wheelchair, fell and broke his hip. More than just his bone shattered.

He was at such a late stage of Alzheimer's that there was no hope of his ever walking again: had he been able to follow even the sim-plest instructions, this prospect might have at least been remotely possible, but he was beyond the reach of language. Indeed, whenever nurses moved him to change him, clean him, make his bed, he held on to any available railing or chair or table as if he were being pried off a life raft by an army of malevolent demons: he was terrified, unknowing, lost, alone. Over the weeks as Virginia began truly to register that Herman would never leave the hospital again, much less walk under his own steam, she made her slow private peace with "reality," a part of which was acknowledging that she herself was in physical pain, more every day. Although she had kept the diagnosis from most of her friends—and right after Herman fell and broke his hip, she was silent about it to everybody—she now had to deal with a growing and in some ways ironic agony: not two weeks before her insentient husband fell and broke his own hip, her doctor had told her that she needed a hip replacement operation. His accident had temporarily wiped out the possibility of her going to the hospital for her own operation, not least because she had to spend nearly every waking hour filling out masses of bureaucratic forms to apply and qualify for public benefits to pay for all of this sudden medical care and hospitalization for Herman as well as herself. For many weeks she was somehow able to will herself to ignore the growing ache in her hip. But after two or three months, it was taking her a good hour to get out of bed—the simplest tasks had become agonizing. She had a son who lived alone in a nearby city, but it was contrary to her temperament to rely on him or anyone else: plus, she knew he was going through a bad time professionally, and she didn't want to impose on him. Indeed, she did not hold much hope that help was to be had from any quarter—she hadn't bothered to look into the help she might have gotten from home aides, to which Medicare entitled her. Instead, she pored over her accounts and mentally parceled out the sum she'd probably have to pay herself, dividing it between nursing home costs for Herman and hospital costs and living expenses. Before she was finished with a morning's worth of figuring, she realized that her assets would not last longer than six months—seven, if she were lucky.

During all of this time, Virginia prayed—she was always conscious of her faith in God, and she continued to believe that help was at least possible from angels, in whose beneficent agency she had believed ever since she was a little girl. She envisioned these angels mostly as deceased relatives and close friends who she somehow felt were pulling for her. But lately their help seemed to be much more distant, much less dramatic. As she went every day to spoon Herman's lunch into his mouth and saw his slowly disappearing smile—he had long since ceased to recognize her—and felt the pain intensify into her own limbs, she began to think, really, that even her angels had deserted her. They were the souls, after all, of people who had died so long ago. Surely they'd long moved on to younger people, people who needed more immediate help, with lives they'd only just begun. Virginia was clearly at the end of her run. Herman had traveled even farther into the growing dark of his future.

By this time Virginia had made some quiet plans for her hip replacement operation—she'd completed most of the bureaucratic red tape about financing. She didn't expect to live all that much longer herself, but how could she care for herself if she couldn't walk? Never one used to complaining about pain, she finally had no choice but to schedule the operation and ensuing rehab. But she didn't push it—when the hospital called to say they would have to postpone for a couple of weeks, she meekly acquiesced.

But one morning she couldn't get out of bed. The pain was so intense, she couldn't even turn to reach for the phone—her only imaginable recourse to get help. She waited for the pain to pass—it always had before, after forty-five minutes, an hour, rarely longer. But every time she breathed, she felt like yelping: this was pain unlike any other she could remember—worse, it even seemed to her, than giving birth. What could she do? She prayed for strength. None came. She prayed for guidance of any kind. No voice harkened to her—her angels, it seemed, had deserted her. She began to cry. She hadn't cried for so long. She had never felt such an extreme despair. She almost mouthed the words she thought she'd never say: she almost prayed for death.

But just as her despair seemed to draw her down into some terrible dark abyss in her soul—just as she felt she couldn't go on one moment longer—some small voice inside her gently asked her to stop, and breathe, and relax. "I don't know where it came from. It wasn't like I'd asked for help from any spiritual source. But it did feel like an angel. And what this angel began to tell me—really it was more by helping me to feel, than by speaking to me in language—what this voice allowed me to feel was the huge need to be *cleansed.* I can't think of another word for it.

"I knew in that moment that what was poisoning me—what was toxic for me right at that moment—wasn't so much the pain in my hip, or the extremity of despair I'd reached, not believing that anyone could come to my aid. The toxin was doubt, fear—a kind of negative expectation I didn't even realize I had! I mean, when I think of the need for 'purity,' I tend to think of sinners out of the Bible who need to change their selfish hedonistic ways. But that's not the kind of purity that was being called for here.

"I was poisoning myself by not trusting in the abundance of help available to me. I saw that in my determination to 'do it all myself,' I was really being very arrogant. I needed help—the Universe, and my angels, wanted me to have help. To have turned my back away from the source of this needed help was not only foolish but prideful. Somehow, something released in me, and though I still wasn't able yet to reach for the phone, my pain abated a little, and I allowed myself to fall back on the bed and receive what felt like a cleansing wave from this angel, this messenger. Angels are messengers—that became so clear to me. They do after all bring 'glad tidings.' They want me to know that I don't have to struggle so very, very hard."

As Virginia lay back on her bed, as she surrendered to this detoxifying wave from the Angel of Purity, the phone rang. Now, when she reached for it, her pain had lessened, and she could pick it up. It was her son. He told her how worried he was about her, and how he was planning to help her pack and get ready for her operation that weekend. Her old impulse would have been to ward him off, to make it appear that she'd be fine on her own and really didn't need his help, especially with all the business difficulties she knew he was having. But somehow that purifying wave changed Virginia. She thanked him, simply. She accepted his offer of help. She told him she loved him. In other words, she stopped resisting—and as she registered the palpable, physical feeling of letting go that she now allowed herself, she realized how tense she'd normally been. Her whole life now seemed as if it had been one fearful, white-knuckled attempt to "hold on."

Virginia may have appeared, on the face of it, to be the sweetest and most moral and from some points of view the "purest" of human beings one could hope to meet—and yet she had kept herself locked from the abundant help her angels wanted her to have. She identified her own "toxins" of which she needed to be cleansed: doubt and fear. In releasing them, amazing things have begun to happen. Friends she hadn't heard from in years have emerged and offered to help. She's discovered she's entitled to much more financial help than she'd dared to hope. She's even discovered that Herman is entitled to a more comfortable quarter of the nursing home. All of this has come as if through a channel that the Angel of Purity helped her to clear. All Virginia had to learn to do was "detox"—rid herself of self-imposed limits and fearful ideas that "there would never be enough and I'll have to do it all myself," none of which had any relation to the abundant reality that awaited her—the abundant clarity that the Angel of Purity has now bestowed on her.

The clarity that the Angel of Purity offers is twofold: clarity of purpose, and clarity of trust. This angel wants us to focus as purely as we can on our best, least complicated motives—our least ego-ridden intentions—so that our aims are as innocent and unfettered as they can be. But the clarity of trust is just as important: indeed, the whole thrust of this chronology of angels—and the steps they personify—might be said to illuminate and bring us closer to the ability to trust, to trust absolutely. Clarity of purpose, coupled with simple, "pure" trust: this is the gift the Angel of Purity truly offers.

This angel also, unmistakably, acquaints us with a clearer sense of the "divine." I have not talked about "God" here because we each have such an individual take on the nature of God, what God means.

But in whatever way you feel disposed to conceive of God, the Angel of Purity beckons you to make conscious contact with this divine presence—as simply and directly as a child seeks contact with a loved parent. This angel tells you to "keep it simple." Be clear, trust, open up to the abundance—let God's love, through the messenger of this angel, comfort and guide you.

But heed the wake-up call of this angel as well. Another restaurateur client of mine had a very ambitious "theme" scheme for his restaurant, and he was off to the races with an impressive vision and a wonderful series of willing partners. In fact, he seemed to be careening into a great success with lightning speed. The money started to come in, he spent a great deal of it on very expensive trappings and décor, overbooked the place, overspent, started to lose the confidence of some of his partners, began to get haughty and egotistical just when he needed to ask for help—and his whole top-heavy restaurant and club, which once looked like the picture of spectacular success, suddenly looked like it might come to an abrupt and unhappy halt.

This gentleman, Andrew, came back to me right at this shaky moment—and it was quickly evident to me that he was not clear about his motives, about what he wanted his business to be. He needed to call upon the Angel of Purity, to achieve that clarity of aim and simple trust. With the renewed focus and simplicity that the Angel of Purity was able to give him—and can give us—we're able to ask for and receive a more powerful source of strength and stamina than we've ever known before.

6

THE ANGEL OF STRENGTH

By now you have the clue that, in the realm of angels, *strength* probably means something significantly different from most of its conventional definitions. What do we normally think of when we hear the word *strength?* Bodily strength—strength of character—the strength of a material such as metal or wood or wire: whether emotional or physical, most definitions of the word connote something that is in some way forcibly *exerted.*

The gift of strength as it's offered by the Angel of Strength has many quite different qualities. Just as "the quality of mercy is not strained," the quality of angelic gifts is never strained either. There is always a free flow to the communion that angels have with us, and to the ways in which they embrace and help us. Strength as it's purveyed by this angel is intrinsic, unforced, instantly available to everyone. It has a spiritual quality: it flows through all things; it doesn't need to be pushed or pulled and it won't run out.

The Angel of Strength wants you to know three essential truths, all of which draw on a special understanding of "strength":

1. You are a powerful being.
2. You deserve what you desire in life.
3. It is never too late to start.

Of these, it would appear that only the first ("You are a powerful being") is explicitly about "strength." But knowing that you deserve what you desire—and knowing that it is never too late to start on the pursuit of what you desire—also intrinsically beckons to the Angel of Strength to give you the wherewithal not only to get started but to sustain your energy as you pursue your desire.

We saw in the Angels of Vision and Wisdom the importance of "intention": without it, we'll just bump into walls. Imagine going to an airport with a blank ticket: how confusing and pointless the place would seem! Vision and Wisdom acquaint us with our first clear view of what we want in life; the Angel of Purity helps us polish that view so that we know we're being honest with ourselves about what we really want: the trait of purity helps us to identify and discard the more purely ego-ridden (fearful, envious, prideful) motives so that they don't get in our way. The Angel of Strength comes to our aid now because we are ready for it: we truly do know what we want by the time we call upon its aid. This angel comes to us to make sure that our intention is "set," and that we have the energy and the passion and the resources to follow it through.

To sustain this kind of energy—to draw on this kind of unforced freely given "strength"—we do profit from focusing on each of the three "essential truths" that the Angel of Strength wants us to keep in mind. It's helpful to see how they provide conduits to the strength that is this angel's gift.

For example, the first assertion: "You are a powerful being."

This is one of the most perfect examples of an angelic mantra: it does not say you will be a powerful being, or that you could be a powerful being, or that if you did this or that thing you would find out that you're a powerful being. You *are* one. Simply by repeating it to yourself—with an "I" ("I am a powerful being")—you already participate in the gift. You are powerful now! This is how this angel's gift comes to us—effortlessly, as if it had always been there to begin with (which of course it has).

The Angel of Strength floods us with power, simply as we repeat this mantra. One woman who came to see me discovered this fact with almost hilarious suddenness. Arianne had taught elementary school for about ten years but secretly wanted to write and stage inventive comic plays for kids, which she envisioned taking from town to town and school to school—with an itinerant band of actors and clowns who'd turn whatever stage they mounted into a party. Having been brought up in a very strict family and gone to a school that was equally severe and humorless, Arianne had long been brewing some pretty iconoclastic children's plays in her imagination: she was determined to help other kids enjoy learning in ways she never had. But all those years of having to toe the line with family and hyperdisciplined schoolteachers had left her a little shell-shocked and shy. She had all sorts of wonderful ideas, and she had contacted a number of actors who were interested, and she even had some leads to various local boards of education that would very likely be receptive—but she couldn't make that first call. I had already helped her to make contact with the Angels of Vision and Wisdom and to ask for help in staying on track from the Angel of Purity. By this time, she had a complete script and group of committed actors and a very persuasive spiel about how beneficial the children's play would be in any school. But she still was terrified of making the first move: talking to a principal just stoked too many awful memories of her stern school-teachers.

She was, however, bursting to do it: she obviously ached for some clue about how to get over this hump of fear. I offered her the Angel of Strength's first mantra, asked that she say it with all her heart and mind and soul. Arianne is a tiny woman—slightly built, barely five feet—and normally very quiet. So I was not prepared for the lion's roar that came out when she repeated: *I am a powerful being!*

She *was* a powerful being! And on the strength of this assertion, she picked up the phone, got right through to the elementary school principal she'd wanted to talk to, and—well, I don't know when I've heard a warmer, smoother, more assured, more authentically heart-felt pitch than the one I heard Arianne make right then on that phone. She was radiant with strength—but not the "strength" of white-knuckled, fearful exertion. It was freely accepted, given, joyous: a kind of emotional "fuel" to which she had only to open herself to receive as much as she needed.

This may sound too good to be true, but perhaps it bolsters credibility to make an important point about Arianne's receptivity here—and anybody's receptivity to an angel's gifts. Arianne realized that her previous gifts of Vision, Wisdom, and Purity all created a kind of space in which she could call upon the Angel of Strength for help. "It's not that it didn't take courage," she says. "I still have a horror of picking up the phone and speaking to 'authorities.' But I'd done the spadework. I was so confident about the children's program I wanted to stage—I had done all the work I'd needed to do to make the thing plausible to the school powers-that-be, all of which were products of

Vision, Wisdom, and Purity—that when I took the scary leap of picking up the phone (after asking this Angel of Strength for help), it
wasn't so much scary as exhilarating! I was ready. And I know it
sounds weird talking about these angels in such a stilted way—or
their gifts in such stilted ways—Vision, Wisdom, Purity, and Strength
almost sound like names of Puritan girls in *The Crucible!*—but my
beckoning to them is actually silent, private. It's something sort of
just between me and the angel-in-question. It's actually a very inti-
mate connection."

It often seems that we're able to take in and embrace a particular
angel's gift only as completely as we've been able to take in previous
gifts in the "progression." We may learn this lesson awkwardly—
sometimes by imagining we can skip the gifts of, say, "purity" or
"strength"—only to find that something really crucial has been left
out of the mix. But when we're really ripe for a particular angelic gift,
as Arianne was for that "I am a powerful being" mantra, look out!
Make way for some immediate dramatic miracles!

The second mantra, "You deserve what you desire in life," also
beckons to the Angel of Strength to flood you with power—again,
effortlessly; again, as freely and generously as you've got the capacity to receive. There are two powerful words in this assertion:
deserve and *desire;* together, they create the most powerful possible
agent for change: with the certainty that you deserve, and the passion of desire, there's simply nothing you can't do. Once again, this
assertion beckons to the gift of strength *intrinsically:* you find it's
already there before you've asked for it!

It's a tough mantra for a lot of people, however: the notion that
we "deserve" what we "desire" is not one we commonly grow up

believing. If our angels sometimes cry for us out of frustration, it's surely because of this central mistake in our thinking. *Deserve* and *desire* are not greedy verbs: they're abundant verbs. There's no end to the gifts we are given, nothing that ever need stop the flow of what these angels want us to have.

Virginia—the 82-year-old lady we met in our discussion of the Angel of Purity—has needed to learn this lesson perhaps more than any other. We saw her resist the idea not only that help was to be had (with her operation, planning for her husband, financing her medical treatments, and so on) but that she was *entitled* to it, and that the entrenched (fearful) certainty that she couldn't be helped was from one point of view presumptuous, a kind of arrogance. Alas, so many of us grow up thinking it's "good" not to have what we want, that we build character by depriving ourselves of what we love. Far from "building character," this mind-set actually erodes our happiness and our soul's expansiveness. Once again, the simplicity of this mantra calls up the gift of strength from the angel before we've blinked: "I deserve what I desire." Simply saying that clears the channel—and before long, what you desire will materialize, and you will embrace it with the wholehearted pleasure of knowing you deserve it. Strength, once again, floods in: it's already *here.*

The third mantra, "It's never too late to start," is also a powerful one, even if it also appears to draw through the back door the strength this angel wants us to have. Free-flowing energy and strength and purpose—and *intention*—aren't something you can summon up only when you're young or in the morning or when you're sure you'll have time to get it all done: this kind of energy and strength is eternal. Our angels want us to know that miracles are normal. Expect everything. Or, maybe more profitably, shed all expectations! "It's never too late to start" isn't just a nice reminder that you can effect change in your life whenever you want: it's a subtle way of reminding you that you are always in eternity. You can start a brilliant work of art at 95; you can come up with a poem in fifteen minutes that may win a literary prize; you can express the most profoundly nurturing love to someone full of despair in the space of a few seconds. We commune and create with great force and effect all the time: we are as capable of joyous connection at 11:30 P.M. at the end of a long day as we are at 6:30 A.M. after a long night's restful sleep. We pretend we are the prisoners of time, but we aren't. We have the strength, as this angel's gift, to transcend all boundaries. Everything is possible, this angel—all these angels—want us to know.

LIFE FORCE

Think of these angels—in fact, all of the angels in your life—as joyous, eager messengers who can't wait to let you know the good news they bring. As you allow this progression of angels to give you their gifts and help you with their power, you'll find that the benefits you derive from them are always deeper and more profound than they first appear. The Angel of Strength is a good example: you may still think of "strength" in a limited way, even now, even as you ask this angel for it: "Oh, please give me the fortitude to last through the rest of my workday," or "Please give me the stamina to finish this project by the deadline"—all perfectly reasonable requests of this angel, and yet all reflecting only the barest surface of the "strength" that is to be had.

The Angel of Strength offers you nothing less than the life force. Ultimately, this angel wants us to know that this force is infinite—and to learn to use so much more of it than you usually do. When this angel says to us, "You are a powerful being," we generally don't have a clue just *how* powerful. The strength we're offered is *the strength of life itself,* the unstoppable impelling force that keeps us alive, allows us to connect to each other, and ultimately enables us to make contact with God. There is nothing this force can't do.

Strength from this angel is never "imminent," about to happen. It's always "immanent": it *is* now, it is already everywhere, it floods through you and the Universe. You have only to trust that it's there to make use of it. The strength to trust is, in fact, a large dividend of what this angel offers. I was told by my guardian angel that I would never be able to "read" myself psychically—to see my own future, as I'm often able to "see" what awaits my clients. At first I thought, what kind of "gift" is this, that I can't apply to myself? But not being able to sense things psychically about myself has turned into the greatest part of my gift, a gift I credit to the Angel of Strength. I am forced to trust the evolution of life and growth I have been offered. The Angel of Strength gives me the stamina and the certainty to renew this trust at the many moments I still feel vulnerable.

The immense spiritual power this angel offers us was vividly brought home to me recently when I received word of a friend—a mother with three kids—who was driving through Sardinia on a month-long trip through the Mediterranean. It was rainy, and the coastal roads were slippery, unlit, and dangerous—so dangerous that the car my friend was driving slid off the road, flipping over again and again into a ravine, and bouncing off a rocky cliff—all of which ought

to have totaled the car and killed this woman and her three daughters. But right when she felt the car go out of control, this woman somehow had the spiritual presence of mind to ask for the strength, the life force, to exert control over the outcome of the crash. She's careful now to say she asked for it, not demanded it: it was a kind of prayer. But she knew that what she had full access to was the most powerful force on the planet: the force of life. She felt that the Angel of Strength had granted her "use" of this life force. Her motive was so purely to save the lives of her children—her motive was so purely love—that she almost wasn't surprised when she and her kids were able to get out of the car at the bottom of the ravine. She had made the connection between strength and love—and recognized in that moment of grace when their lives had been spared that they were in fact the same thing. There is no greater strength than love.

Which is why the Angel of Love comes in the progression when it does: now.

7

THE ANGEL OF LOVE

The genius of this angelic progression is how caringly and inventively it encourages you to grow. You are invited to receive a new angel's gifts precisely at the moment when you're most receptive to them—which is also usually the moment you most need to receive them. What you want—if it's the product of your deepest vision and desire—is always also what you need. A friend of mine says he needs to remind himself of this every day: taped to the inside of his front door (so he can't miss it when he leaves for work in the morning) is a three-by-five card with his own handwritten words: "What you want, wants you." This is so much more profoundly true than most people realize.

Of course, you've been coaxed down the path to realizing this truth all along, even by angels you didn't know existed or whose help you haven't yet specifically requested. The Angel of Love has never been far off in your life. This angel has always tried to guide you, reassure you, help you to make contact with what is, after all, the most powerful force in the Universe. But now that you are finally ready to *focus* on the gift of love this angel offers, *all* your angels rejoice. All know how much more can happen in your life when you become more conscious of the love that is eternally available to you—and available through you to others.

But first take a moment to take stock. Think of the progress you've made with the help of all the angels you've consciously let into your heart and mind: think of the legacy you have allowed them to bestow! A sense of vision that connects you to the world and feeds your soul, a growing inward acceptance of who you are—all the focus, clarity, and strength you need to do anything you want to do.

As wonderful as this whole angelically derived apparatus is—as efficient and powerful a mechanism for realizing your dreams these angelic lessons prove to be—without love, none of it has any real meaning. Strength without love can be monstrous. Vision without love is often cold and self-serving. Indeed, none of the angelic gifts you've been offered can benefit you for very long without the "juice" of love. If you've freely accepted your angels' gifts, you probably already know this. Pursuing even what may first have struck you as "selfish" goals—say, making more money, or getting a more exciting job, home, car, or wardrobe—always eventually connects you with a larger perspective, the sense not only that you deserve what you desire but that it is karmically "right" for you to pursue it. Getting it will make you more likely to connect to other people. Abundance lifts you, lightens you, makes you more receptive to the world. Without quite having planned it, you suddenly find yourself eager to help others as you've been helped. Not out of some humorless moral obligation—you do it because you can't keep yourself from doing it: your sense of joy is contagious—you want to pass it on!

So an underlying flow of love from your angels has been animating your quest all along. But now that you're ready to encounter the Angel of Love more directly—to look at your own capacity to love, and to ask for whatever help you may need to increase the flow of love in your life—look out. Whatever miracles you may feel have already happened to you will pale against the power and beauty of what awaits you now.

THE SECRET OF FINDING A SOUL MATE

Carrie, at 34, is a beautiful dark-haired woman who very quickly began to enjoy the gifts of all the angels we've so far met. Almost from our first session, she "got" the connection I told her was eternally available to her—the connection between her deepest desires and the resources available to her to make those desires a reality. In the space of six months, with angelic help, she was wooed away from a job in advertising that she felt was holding her back to a job writing for major travel magazines and airlines, which not only gave her far more money than she'd ever made before but enabled her freely to do what she most yearned to do: jet around the world to exotic places. "Ever since I was a child, cooped up in a small Ohio town, I've wanted to see the world. I'm seeing more of it now than I ever thought possible," she says.

But jetting around the world did not make it easy for her to connect for long with a man. Attractive, educated, and accomplished, Carrie found it easy enough to meet men—she'd had a number of romantic liaisons with interesting artists and bohemians and writers throughout her travels. But as interesting as they often were, almost all of them were also weak and unreliable. "I've been raking myself over the coals for whatever pattern I seem stuck in—gravitating to one irresponsible man after another," Carrie told me. "And I know that's not helpful. Beating myself up for some psychological problem I've decided I have just keeps me stuck." Having been helped so profoundly by all the other angels (from Vision to Strength), she was sure that the answer lay in petitioning the next angel on the list: the Angel of Love.

She proceeded to do this conscientiously, faithfully, every night for two, three, four weeks. She meditated every way she knew how. But nothing was happening. No answering response was coming to her, as it had every other time she'd appealed to other angels. It was as if her whole angelic brigade had abandoned her. "I can't believe it," she told me, "but I'm starting to lose faith. What am I doing wrong?"

For some reason I flashed back to my experience in Paris, in Notre Dame. Not so much to the memory of angels cascading down to embrace and reassure me, but rather to the feelings I had had for days before that, walking around the city alone, going to the Louvre, stopping for a cold drink at a café on the Boulevard St-Germain, sitting on the grass in the Bois de Boulogne—seeing a thousand different things that not only told me I was "home" but that I was a gifted, marvelous, blessed creature of God. In other words, I flashed back to the moment when I truly began to love myself, and when I was finally able to see my psychic abilities as gifts rather than afflictions. I realized it was only because I had learned to love and value myself that my Notre Dame angelic revelation had happened at all. The real key to that Parisian epiphany wasn't so much the outcome of having met and learned more about these angels, but rather what I had done to prepare for that outcome. I had learned to love myself.

This was Carrie's challenge as well. And it was a subtle dilemma. Carrie wasn't any obviously self-hating or tortured woman. She was capable of great good sense in every aspect of her professional life: her brilliant success as a writer and travel expert was the product and the proof of this. She had many friends, a full life all around. But when I looked into her eyes, when I saw the pain in them as she asked me "What am I doing wrong?" I remembered looking into a mirror at my own eyes when, back in college, all I could think of doing in the face of any difficulty was to "tune out." Yes, "tuning out"—for example, when I swam—acquainted me with a vast and powerful meditative oasis to which I resort today: it had and has its important uses. But I was able, listening to Carrie, to see that it had also—before that Parisian moment of learning to value who I was—been a way of escaping problems I didn't want to know I had. And the most debilitating of these problems was a lack of true self-regard, self-love.

But how could I tell her this without worsening the problem? If you don't love yourself, being told you don't love yourself rarely helps: it just makes you dislike yourself more for not loving yourself! This problem will not yield to frontal assault. And then I remembered something it had been very hard for Carrie to tell me some weeks before.

"Have you been in contact with Jeff?" I asked her. Carrie's face tensed. She had confided to me how awful her relationship with her brother Jeff was. "He's the most insensitive lout I've ever known," she'd said. "And when our father died, and he refused to come to the funeral, he nearly killed my mother. He's the most selfish, self-involved jerk I've ever known. And it tears me apart, because when we were little—he's two years older than I—he was my best friend, my only confidant! It's like this wonderful soul mate suddenly turned into a demon. I don't know what his bitterness and rage are all about, but I can't stand to be around him anymore. Jeff's first reflex seems to be to lash out, to hurt. I won't let myself be hurt by him anymore." Carrie told me she hadn't talked to him in five years.

Now, when I asked her about him, Carrie shuddered involuntarily. She was silent for a moment. Then quietly she spoke: "Funny you should ask. I've been having dreams about him. Dreams about climbing into the treehouse we built for ourselves when we were kids. Dreams about hiding up there away from everyone else—the excitement that kids feel when they're 'spying' on the rest of the world. They've been wonderful dreams. The first time in years I've thought of him with love. It just makes me sadder when I wake up and realize how far from that loving bond we now are."

I suggested to Carrie that she call Jeff. "Don't write—that's too much of an invitation to defend and keep him at arm's length. Just call him to see how he is."

Carrie was terrified by the prospect, but at the same time it intrigued her. She was also intrigued that I evidently thought it would help unblock her romantically. "How will that help?" she asked. I had my ideas on the topic but decided to remain enigmatic. "I don't know," I said. "I just think it's a good idea." Carrie had built up enough internal strength and resolve (remember, she had employed the gifts of most of the angelic progression now for quite some time) to be able to realize she could deal with whatever happened at the other end of the phone. But just before she left me to go home and make the call, her anxiety returned in a brief blast. She turned around to face me, worried: "What should I say to him?" I made the deepest eye contact I could with her. "Anything that comes to mind," I said, repressing a chuckle. At the same time I spoke, I heard a congratulatory bark of psychic laughter in my head.

Apparently the Angel of Love approved.

Carrie called Jeff and then phoned me to say it was a revelation. "At first he sounded like the old Jeff—his usual rude greeting: 'What do you want?' An answer popped out of my mouth before I had a chance to stop it: 'I want to reconnect with you, Jeff. I miss you.'"

Carrie said she thought the line went dead—and then she heard a deep sigh from her brother. It was as if Jeff were a dam waiting to burst: "All he needed was this go-ahead. He said he'd felt awful about the way he'd turned his back on me, on our family. He confessed that he'd been heavy into drugs when my dad died. It was somehow his twisted sense of guilt that kept him from the funeral. Well, he also didn't want anyone to see how down and out he was." Carrie paused. "I don't mean to say it was all sweetness and light. He feels a lot of bitterness about the way our parents treated him—he spent a lot of time venting at me, all but accusing me of being 'on their side.' But something inside told me to keep quiet, just listen, let him say whatever he needed to say. And then—well, I shifted gears. Again, I found myself talking almost without willing it: I'm not sure where my words were coming from. But out of the blue, I started to tell him about the dreams I'd been having. The treehouse, the sense of excitement and fun we had escaping up into it. He started to laugh, remembering. We must've spent an hour in totally uninhibited recall of our childhood. He remembered stuff I didn't, I remembered stuff he didn't, and for that time we became the 8-year-old and 10-year-old we'd been back then. It was like, out of nowhere, we rediscovered the magic of our childhood. Maybe he wasn't the only dam that wanted to burst. There was so much inside me that needed to come out. I didn't realize how desperately I'd missed him until I called him last night."

Carrie paused. "But," she began, "remind me again how this is going to improve my romantic life?" She laughed softly. It was a pleasure to hear her laugh about a topic to which she'd only ever brought anxiety and despair before.

I thought again of Paris, and how what seemed most important to me about the memory was what led up to meeting the angels, not the meeting itself. What is it that makes us receptive? What is it exactly that prepares the way for change? It's as if our angels hover about with great alertness waiting for the first signs of softening, of receptivity, of openness—and then (as they had for me in Notre Dame) they cascade joyfully down to help us go the rest of the distance.

It was Carrie's humor that marked the change for her. What was it a change to? Talking to Jeff for the first time in five years, allowing the hate and fear and mistrust to evaporate—connecting, in other words, with her deep but buried love for her brother—caused a ripple effect in her life. Within days, she was treating everyone— friends, colleagues, her dry cleaner—with a new humor, curiosity. It was as if she were noticing that everyone was human! "I feel like an idiot," Carrie told me a few days later. "I mean, I look around, I see all these lost and lonely and angry and shut-up people, and I think— Wow! Look at them! Look at how many people have felt the way I feel!" Except Carrie no longer felt quite so lost, lonely, angry, and shut up. In releasing her love for her brother, she released her love across the board. She was funnier, kinder, more attentive, more interested in people around her. The love in her wanted to come out: that's perhaps the simplest way of describing it.

Eventually it drew her to an editor at one of the magazines for which she wrote—an editor who was so impressed by her style and expertise that he wanted her to do a column. "The first thing I noticed about him," Carrie said, "was his self-confidence. I realized in that moment that every man I'd met or been involved with before had *winced* a lot. It was like the world scared them, attacked them, made them feel like they had to hide. I don't know, maybe that's how I felt about myself, too. But Mark—that's his name—just sort of stands there like he knows he deserves to stand there! He's not darting away from things, from people. He looks like he knows who he is and what he wants. I'm a little weirded out by it all—I'm not used to someone this 'solid.' We've started to date. We have an incredibly good time. It makes me wonder when the other shoe will drop. But—oh, I should tell you this," she wedged into the conversation. "The Angel of Love is answering me these days. I guess my angels didn't abandon me after all. And what does the angel tell me? 'Lighten up. Let it happen. Don't worry so much.' So I'm trying to do that. And when I can't, I pick up the phone and talk to Jeff, and try to remember another funny thing that happened when we were kids."

When I think of Carrie's openness, the evolution of my own receptivity, and the experiences of so many other men and women I know who've become vulnerable just when they needed to, I'm struck by what an essentially simple process healing is. Carrie didn't launch into a long self-analysis about the neurotic family or childhood roots of why she was attracted so habitually to weak, irresponsible men. When, gently, she was reminded where her love was most blocked, she had the courage to face it: she called her brother to dislodge that block. Releasing this backed-up love for her brother had a domino effect of releasing it elsewhere in her life.

Many clients come to me with tales of romantic woe, certain that they'll never meet "the right person." By reflex they put the blame for their loneliness on some imaginary "right person" who for some reason rudely refuses to materialize. But this is not how to find love. *You find love by loving.* Carrie became receptive to meeting Mark because she had become more receptive to *life.* She was radiant with a new, softer, more beckoning self. She didn't have to look for Mark. She didn't have to look for anyone. She just had to *be.* Now that she had made herself available to the world, Mark would—and (easily) did— find her on his own.

Love is not something to parcel out in meager portions, to withhold from people until they prove themselves worthy of it. We need to feel and express love the way the Angel of Love feels and expresses it for us: bountifully, without question. We need to realize that we can bring love to everything and everyone in our lives, and that doing so will improve everything in our lives. It might sound simplistic, but a good answer to virtually any problem you'll ever face consists of two words: *love more.*

SEEK AND YE WON'T FIND (AT LEAST IF YOU'RE DESPERATE...)

There's seeking and there's seeking. From the first angel we met in this parade, the Angel of Vision, we learned that grabbing at a "picture" of something we think we want won't get us very far: that kind of needy, desperate seeking rarely gets us anything more than a short-term relief or solution.

Then there's the seeking of a child: open, trusting, curious, loving, with few expectations of how anything "ought" to turn out. This kind of seeking is itself a kind of meditation, a way of keeping the psychic pores open so that you can take in whatever you need to take in to move forward. It leads us to the most compelling intentions we can know, intentions born of the heart and spirit whose life and specificity guarantee that they will manifest.

Generative vision requires meditation, patience, and trust to transform into a generative intention. However, when we're hungry for human contact, wary that we'll ever find it, afraid we'll be rejected every time we reach out for it, the "intention" we come up with can be a barren, strangled, and limited thing. We start to decide how the intention ought to be fulfilled—in fact, sometimes we won't settle for fulfillment unless it happens in the particular way we've decided is "right" for us. Not surprisingly, this anxiety impedes us. We strangle our "intentions" when we require that they manifest in a certain way. It's as if we're dying of thirst, but we'll accept water only if we're offered it in a particular cracked, unwashed Fred Flintstone glass. Woe be to the Good Samaritan (or angelic) passerby who offers us Perrier in Baccarat crystal, or fresh spring water out of a cold silver dipper. We won't have any of that. It isn't Fred and Wilma with the chipped rim.

Our angels tell us again and again that there are infinite ways for a dream to be made reality. In fact, it's when we let go of our fearfully limited expectations that our dreams have the best chance of manifesting. A friend of mine has what he calls his Cat Theory of

Human Relationships. As with cats, if you grab at people, he says, people will bolt. They'll see you as a potential jailer. You have to let them come to you. Once they do so—out of their own volition and in their own sweet time—you know they want to be with you. They will have come freely out of affection and love—they are with you because they want to be. You haven't trapped them. You've opened your arms to them. This is not a bad way to think about love.

It recalls the acronym—TAB (Take Action Being)—we looked at back in Chapter 2. "Be"—then "act." Regard the world, take it in, make peace with its reality and with your own mind and heart, expect the best: *then* take the action your mind and heart suggest.

Quiet down, make the connection, ask for help, take action, and let it go.

Peter, a rock guitarist in his late twenties with a vested interest in protecting his macho "kickass" persona, and great pride in his ability to "make it" with any woman he wanted ("The badder I am, the more chicks I get"), didn't have much truck with this approach when I suggested it to him. Peter had been in a fairly successful rock band that opened for bigger groups and actually allowed him to make a pretty good living, unlike most of his rocker friends, who still worked at gas stations and played in garages. He'd come to me not for anything to do with "spiritual growth" but because he'd heard I'd helped a lot of people "realize their dreams"—which equated in Peter's mind with "make a ton of money and get famous." Tense, tight, sullen: every word that came out of him sounded like a challenge. "Don't try any of that New Age shit on me," he said. "I just wanna be a rock star."

I told Peter I'd be delighted to help him make a ton of money and get famous. I talked to him about these angels, and how he would need to ask for their help—starting with the Angel of Vision, working through Wisdom, Purity, Strength, Love—and Peter stopped me. "Love?" He snorted like a horse. "Who said anything about love? Just tell me how to get my band off the ground."

When I made the suggestion to Carrie to call her brother and she asked me, "What do I say to him?" a voice I identified as the Angel of Love laughed approvingly at the moment I said, "Whatever comes to mind!" Well, something similar happened now. As I looked at this scowling young man, I smiled, and heard in my head: *"Go get him!"* The voice told me that Peter was ripe for revelation. He may have thought he'd come purely to make it big in the rock world, but the Angel of Love told me he'd come for much more. This was one isolated, withdrawn young man. The angel he most wanted to dismiss was, of course, the angel he most needed to embrace.

Over the next few sessions, I tried to help Peter focus on the vision he wanted for his band. But it was difficult. We cannot make contact with these angels if we're not willing to let go, become in some way spiritually humble and open. It was a while before Peter realized that he could not demand help from the world: he had to ask for it and stay as open as he could to whatever answers came. It finally clicked for him in our third session. At first I wasn't sure why. I was leading him in a guided meditation and expecting his usual frown, when suddenly his brow relaxed, and a bit more light came into his eyes. "Ah," he said. "I see." What did he see, I asked him? "Janet," he said.

 "For some reason, I just remembered this chick Janet I knew back in high school," Peter told me. "I was so turned on by her. She wasn't like any girl I'd ever known. She wasn't a pushover for rock stars, for one thing. But she came to all my band's gigs. She obviously liked the music. What I couldn't understand is why she just didn't turn into one more groupie. I had plenty of those by the time I was seventeen. Once I called her on it. 'You wanna go out?' I asked her at the end of one club date—she'd come with some of her girlfriends. She looked at me, surprised. 'I don't even know you!' she said. 'Well, you listen to enough of my music. That's as good as knowing me.' She laughed. It stung. She wasn't just giving herself to me. 'Takes more than that to know someone,' she said. She pissed me off. I thought, the hell with her, I got plenty of other chicks to play with. So I tried to ignore her. But she kept coming back to hear the band, and whenever she was in the audience, I couldn't keep my eyes from going to her, I couldn't keep myself from aiming my performance at her. She sat there enjoying it, but I could tell I wasn't seducing her the way I wanted to. I tried different tactics. Once I was real nice to her, tried to get her to talk about what kind of music she liked. Once I sent her comp tickets to a gig we had at an expensive club. But nothing I did worked. She just wasn't having any of me. She was just there, she said, because of the music. I couldn't get her out of my mind. I even began"—Peter frowned at himself again—"to sort of pray about it. 'Tell me how to get this chick!' I pleaded with the Great Beyond. But nothing worked. And then one day I found out she'd moved away. It seemed I would never connect with her. I'll tell you, it hurt. I felt—I don't know, like I didn't have any power. It really knocked me flat for a while."

How did this relate to his sudden understanding about "getting humble"? Peter paused for a moment. "I just connected with how I felt back then. I felt real humble. It's like I was silently pleading with her: 'Tell me what to do and I'll do it.' I guess I understand now what you mean about letting go. All I've got to think of is Janet. I felt like an open field where she could've planted anything she wanted to."

Suddenly I had an idea, one I also credit to the ever-vigilant Angel of Love. "Next gig you have," I suggested to Peter, "imagine that Janet's in the audience. Try to reach her with your music." Peter's eyes brightened. "Strange, but I often do that now. Then I kick myself for being a sap and I stop. Why am I still fixated on this girl I knew back in high school? But, okay. I'll try it. I won't stop myself this time."

This began a period of transformation for Peter. His music, he said, was becoming more focused, more intense. As he began to "see" Janet in front of him, he began truly wanting to reach her—reach his audience—with a passionate intent. The vision he'd struggled to come up with for his band now began to take form. He knew he wanted to do a new kind of music—kickass rock, but with more pure emotion in it than kickass rock usually had. Some seed had been planted in him, and it was bearing a strange new creative fruit. "I'm even starting to write love songs," Peter said, a little embarrassed. "It's like, trying to 'reach' Janet feels like trying to reach something in myself—in everyone in the audience. Something—deeper. Maybe even spiritual." Peter groaned: "God, you've brainwashed me," he laughed. "Listen to this New Age crap coming out of me."

The memory of Janet came to Peter without my conscious prodding. It emerged because something deep in him needed it to emerge. The Angel of Love, ever ready, responded to this memory as the buried plea for help it was. The stalemate Peter perceived in his rock career reflected the dead end he secretly felt he'd reached as a man and as a human being. It would not have helped to lecture Peter about his blocked-off ability to feel and express love. All I could do was give him a place where he could allow this recognition to surface in himself, in its own way and time. (Remember that cat theory.)

As with Carrie, it took just this tiny seed to start a whole new forest. Somehow by reflecting on the *symbol* of Janet, Peter has begun a whole new way of looking at himself, his friends, the women in his life, and of course, his band. He's getting more prominent music gigs. He's just been approached to do a record. *Rolling Stone* just did an overview piece about new bands on the horizon, highlighting his as "the one to look out for."

He smiles more. He doesn't wince so much at the sound of the word *love*. He seems a lot more at peace with himself.

Which, not incidentally, is the realm of the angel whose embrace awaits us next.

8

THε ANGεL OF PεACε

Set your goals in life as if you have already attained them. Do not make false divisions between idea and reality, desire and actuality.

In a couple of sentences, this describes what every angel in this progression urges us to do. By now, the remarkable fact that we literally create our lives from our thoughts and beliefs will have registered at least to some degree with all of us. But we've also learned that we need all of these angels' help to keep on track: to remind ourselves to stay fully alert as we create our lives so that we don't sabotage ourselves with old, negative, unconscious reflexes, to make sure that what we manifest is consonant with our true "vision" and that it aligns with a higher good.

"Higher good" may sound a little forbidding, as if I'm suddenly dragging a little bit of Puritan piety into the discussion. In fact, the material prosperity and success these angels joyfully help us to achieve are as wonderful and miraculous as they have always been. We deserve what we desire—and the supply of what we desire is infinite: our angels want us to take as much of it as we want. The "higher good" I'm speaking of isn't in conflict with material wealth and success and pleasure. Nor is it something you need to research in some religious tract or prayer book, or be lectured about by some moral or religious pundit. The "higher good" is in fact *your* "higher good": a larger sense of purpose that you discover and determine for yourself. Why "higher"? The effects of growing in the ways you will have grown, as you register these angels' gifts and counsel more deeply, is to *lift* you, to give you a wider, clearer sense of yourself and of the world. Your capacity to rise up and regard this larger landscape—to understand more about other people's motives and behavior without taking anything too seriously or personally, to feel more compassion toward others—all proceeds from the kind of glorious happy success that the angels help to provide you. It can be said simply: when you're happy and fulfilled, you begin to look outside yourself, and you start to want to help others become happy and fulfilled. Your perspective seems to come from a higher vantage point: you feel "lighter," more effortlessly capable, more likely to see humor in things.

Certainly, guided by the clarity and compassion that have grown naturally as the result of all our angelic lessons and experience, "lightness" characterizes the growing desire to connect with others, to help them, to ease their distress. Spontaneously, inevitably, just by allowing the angels' lessons to register deep within us, and by enjoying all the gifts they bestow, we begin to feel *connected* to the world in profoundly generative ways. We know we're not alone. We discover the deep joy of making a positive difference in other people's lives. Now, especially in the wake of inviting the Angel of Love into our hearts and lives, we generally begin to make more connections between our day-to-day reality and our larger "karmic" purpose on the planet. We begin to take greater joy in *participating* in life, in seeing how what Joseph Campbell called "following your bliss" inevitably *connects* us more deeply and satisfyingly with people.

"Peace" in this context—and certainly the peace that this angel offers—isn't some numbing haze of mindless contentment meant to cushion you from the world. Peace is active and alive, a continually flowing current that both animates and centers you, no matter what you face or feel you need to do. It is fed by—and is to some degree the direct product of—self-knowledge, self-acceptance, and self-love. You cannot know peace until you are clear about and happy with who you are. *Peace comes from within.* When peace proceeds from the deepest wells in you, from true self-love and forgiveness, its miraculous power is unleashed. Like its close relative, love, peace connects you with the greatest forces in the Universe. There's nothing you can't do under its profound and powerful influence.

But remember my description of the "soul party" I sensed was going on among the people I met and the angelic presences I felt in Sun Valley, Idaho? Those blooming, transformative energies, colors, auras, and messages—endlessly varied, lively, joyful...There's abundant *life* in peace, too! Remember how my own angels came down to me in that purple vortex, whirling around my head, twinkling, sparkling, full of an active, eager urgency. Neither encounter was frantic: both simply felt *alive*. There was peace at the heart of each joyful angelic activity—a calming, centering, active, happy peace. It helped me breathe more slowly, open my eyes wider, and want to take in more, not less, of the world.

 As busy and purposeful as a thriving colony, as changeable and evanescent as the colors of sunrise brightening into day, angels participate in the pursuit of helping us with our lives with every last fiber of their beings: they are in a constant state of flux and change as they attempt to help us grow and thrive. But the pervasive feeling even in all this activity is profoundly peaceful. *They are doing what they were created to do.* The peace they radiate comes from a sense of absolute rightness, of complete accord between their activity and their goals: complete alignment with their own "higher good."

Similarly, when we do what (with the angels' help) we discover we were "created" to do, when we feel the same sense of rightness and alignment with our own "higher purposes," we know the same deep, enlivening peace. It is a "peace," as Christian scripture puts it, "which passeth all understanding." It's like having a bit of God inside you.

So "peace" isn't a snooze in the hay. Encouraging us to draw ourselves closer to it, the Angel of Peace enables us to see it as essentially *active* and practical: a fertile state of centered self-acceptance that helps us to engage with the world much more effectively, happily, and profitably. Peace, this angel tells us, is not an escape, a blanket to pull over our heads: it signals that we are living fully—in full alignment with the Universe.

FINDING (AND KEEPING) THE PEACE

"The people I gravitate to have always been the 'ones that got away,'" Doreen says. "The oddballs of their families, the ones who broke free of family expectations and did what they wanted to do." The eldest daughter in a family of three kids and two hardworking parents, Doreen, at 43, was until recently the only one in her family to graduate from college and pursue a profession. She's taught art for fifteen years in a small women's college—after acquiring a Ph.D. in her field.

"My dad and mom died a couple years ago," Doreen says, "and my brother and sister, well—one has a drug problem, and the other needs financial help with grad school. I've become the 'parent' they turn to now. But I still fixate on my childhood when we were still all together and I first tried to emerge as myself. It wasn't easy," Doreen says with a rueful laugh. "They were always funny and bright and loving, but they didn't have a clue what made me tick. I guess some people would call them 'provincial' and 'working class,' but those labels always struck me as elitist snobbery. I went to a fancy Seven Sisters college on a full scholarship, and once I got over being dazed at how accomplished and glamorous and put-together most of my fellow students seemed to be—also how rich!—I felt that my background had prepared me so much better for life than the boarding school summer-in-Switzerland lives that so many of these girls had had. I grew up in one of the grittiest sections of Queens, in New York City. It was a tough life and we never had much money, but then none of my friends did, so that seemed normal. My best friend was a Korean girl who is still my best friend now, all these years later. Melting pot doesn't begin to describe the mix of nationalities and ethnicities—it just came with the territory of living where we lived. Not that everyone got along so well. Far from it. There were gangs, there was bigotry, there was a lot of trouble day to day, but as difficult as it could be, it was so much richer and more varied a world and a life than just about anyone I met in college had experienced. I was always grateful—I still am—for the deep and wide experience my childhood was for me."

But secretly Doreen did feel different from just about everyone else she knew. "I didn't have the same interests as anyone else. I was always attracted to the arts—specifically, from a really early age, seventeenth-century Dutch and Flemish art. I remember being taken to the Metropolitan Museum in elementary school and everyone else was running around the mummies or whining to get into the cafeteria, and there I was, dumbstruck in front of a Vermeer. I couldn't get over the beauty of it. The light, the calm, the purity. That woman pouring water from a pitcher into a bowl. Talk about peace. I was only about nine years old, but I felt like I'd entered some other state of being. I was in a trance." Doreen paused for a second and smiled a little sadly. "A little girl with a fixation on Rembrandt and Vermeer wasn't something even my teachers had ever encountered. Sometimes I'd sneak into the city on the subway so I could go to the Frick Museum and see the Rembrandt self-portraits. I could've stood there all day long just staring at them." She laughs softly. "Sometimes I did.

"So sure, at first I was labeled a weirdo—at least until I learned to hide this crazy art fixation and appear 'normal.' Later on, the 'smart' kids in my high school were all bent on making money as computer whizzes or business magnates. The rest of the kids just wanted to get out of high school. Margaret, my Korean friend, was the only person I knew who had aspirations that reflected my own. She is a brilliant violinist, and she started going to Juilliard's prep school in sixth grade—she'd take the subway in every Saturday morning. I don't know, I guess she felt, like I did about my interest in art, that she had to hide her love of classical music from everybody in school. I think I was the only one of her school friends who knew what she did on Saturdays. We used to joke with each other about it—I mean, it was like we were scurrying away to cop drugs or something, the way we sneaked around! We were sure that people would label us stuck-up because we had such highfalutin interests. It was just so far from what anyone else cared about."

But Margaret had it easier than Doreen in one important way. Margaret's parents—indeed, some of her cousins and other relatives—wholeheartedly encouraged her from the moment, when she was 5, she took an interest in the violin. "Margaret says that half of Juilliard is Asian, usually Korean or Chinese. She almost felt it was her birthright to be there!" While Margaret didn't find any more acceptance at school of her "art" than Doreen, she felt more than compensated for that rejection by the love and acceptance she found at home. "Her parents were always so proud whenever she won a prize or played a concerto," Doreen says. "My family just sort of looked at me dazed. They really didn't understand what I was doing—why I felt so passionate about seventeenth-century Flemish art. I was so smart, supposedly. Why wasn't I pursuing a good solid profession? My dad kept turning the conversation to how much lawyers made."

Doreen *was* lucky, she says, to have her high school art teacher— "an intense, sort of clumsy tall lanky guy who'd gone to Princeton, real brilliant, though the kids didn't like him much because he mumbled all the time. But this public school sure didn't have a lot of Princeton grads, so they bent over backward to keep him. He was something of a trophy, I guess. I became his protégée. At any rate, he encouraged me to read and see exhibitions and even tried to get me a summer work/study thing in Amsterdam right before I went to college. Even with the stipend they offered, it was too expensive. But it was his recommendation that got me into this fancy Seven Sisters school. He really believed in me. Later on he helped me get into graduate school—he followed my career with great care—maybe he saw it as his 'road not taken.' He said, even at seventeen, I had come up with some of the most original and insightful critical writing on art he'd ever read. He made me feel like a prodigy. And while my family didn't quite understand what compelled me to go into art history, they did love me, and they offered me general support. It's funny—one of Margaret's aunts is tone-deaf, and Margaret says that although she always goes with the rest of her family to Margaret's concerts, she sits there looking completely lost. That's kind of what my folks and two sisters and brother looked like when I launched into one of my Vermeer lectures."

Getting to college changed things considerably. "Suddenly I was around people who cared as much as I did about art! It was wonderful. But I noticed, coming home on vacations, that when I'd go on about a wonderful professor or a new friend with whom I was doing a research project, my dad, especially, would just sort of scrunch into his chair and grumble. My mother would glaze over with a lot of 'that's nice, dear's. My sister and brother would just groan. Then, over a Thanksgiving break in my junior year, my brother—he was fifteen then—just blurted out, 'You think you're pretty hot stuff, don't you!'"

Her brother's words stung her, much more deeply and painfully than she says she would ever have expected them to. "I mean, I know he was just being a bratty teenager. But for some reason I couldn't get over the slap. I just looked at him, and I guess I must have looked hurt or baffled because he turned white and apologized. It was such a hostile thing to say. Then I realized why I was having this over-reaction: I could tell he was giving voice to the whole family. I'd been feeling their resentment build up ever since my freshman year. It's like they all thought I'd become this uppity stuck-up coed who talked fancy and felt superior. I was too stunned and hurt to try to talk to them or argue them out of that notion. *I loved them.* Didn't they know that? I was proud of my 'working class' roots: I'd felt I had a leg up on all those rich sweater-and-pearl girls at college: I knew more about the real world than they did. But now I didn't feel like I belonged at home or at college."

Doreen said the rejection she perceived from her family at Thanksgiving stayed with her, even intensified. "When I got back to college, I just felt blah. Gray. I tried to interest myself in a paper about iconography in Dutch interior painting—something I'd been really enthusiastic about when I'd left for Thanksgiving. But now it all just looked like a bunch of old pots and pans and candlesticks. Suddenly *all* art was boring—and nothing so much as all these homey Dutch kitchens and parlors I'd been staring at all my life. What was I spending my education doing? My family was right: this was a self-indulgent waste of time. I should concentrate on getting into law school. Do something useful with my life."

Disgusted with herself—and with what she'd decided was the useless work she'd been doing in art history—Doreen slammed her books and notebooks shut and stormed out of her dorm to take a walk in a neighboring woods. "My anger quickly evaporated: now all I felt was drained and powerless," she says. "But also silly—I mean, it wasn't like I was dealing with cancer or my mother dying or losing a leg in a car accident. Why was I so upset? This was the sort of cross-roads plenty of people in college faced. If I decided I didn't like art history, I could just change majors! It was no big thing." But then, a good quarter-mile down the path into the woods, she stopped. She suddenly felt like she couldn't take another step: she wanted to crumple onto a huge pile of leaves someone had raked by the side of the path. She felt nearly intolerable despair.

She sank into those leaves.

"This was it," she says now, her eyes glistening with the memory. "I suddenly registered—really for the first conscious time in my life— that I had poured the best and highest parts of myself, my greatest gifts, talents, and passions, into this realm of art. It wasn't some fancy academic enterprise to me—it was like I knew what those Dutch and Flemish artists were thinking, what they were trying to do. Really, I regarded them more as my family than my real family back in Queens! And yet I felt so foolish, suddenly, that I'd fallen for all that. But also unspeakably hurt that no one in my family understood how important it was to me! It was like they'd dismissed some part of my soul. How could they love me and not at least try to understand what all this meant to me? But then I thought, maybe they're right, after all. What possible good could studying this do me or anyone else?

"But the pain, the worst of the pain, came from how suddenly my joy had been yanked away from me. It was like all this childlike unquestioned curiosity and pleasure I'd felt my whole life about art just—vanished! There was now a terrible gray chaos where my heart used to be. What was I supposed to do now? I knew my family wanted me to do some 'normal' thing, get off my high horse, join the 'real world.' But I felt completely inadequate. I felt like someone had kicked me hard in the gut. I started to cry. Really sob. I felt as bleak as the late November weather, as dead and empty as the hollowed-out tree trunk I leaned against in the leaves. I cried. I realize now that in some way I was crying for help."

Doreen isn't quite sure how to explain what happened next. "The sky was overcast—that's the crazy thing. I mean, I know that the sun didn't suddenly break through a cloud. It wasn't anything as normal as that! But there was—a hush. And I knew somehow that something was going to reveal itself to me. What? I don't know what I thought—just something. And then"—she looked up at me as if to make sure I wasn't frowning in disbelief (she forgot I'd seen angels, too!)—"there sort of fell down from the trees a slim column of white light. It positioned itself in front of me, like a perfectly vertical but graceful sapling, a sort of tree of light—and the more I looked at it, the more I calmed down. I wish I could say I saw an angel. I didn't. But I felt this amazing *peace.* Perhaps my despair was so great that it somehow created out of thin air exactly what I needed to lessen its severity. But I can't say I 'thought' that then, or much of anything else. No words came to me. Just this growing peace. And it wasn't like, oh I don't know, the 'peace' of looking over a beautiful seascape or other calm and soothing aesthetic panorama. This was deeper. It didn't come from outside me. It didn't even really come from this column of light. It was like the light was just a kind of wake-up call for me, a signal to pay attention. I can't explain it. I only know that something inside me unclenched, let go. And I felt this amazing calm. Not a stupor. I didn't feel like going to sleep. In fact, what went through my mind were vivid, happy images from my childhood—like those times I'd steal away to the Frick—that gorgeous, quiet, sophisticated mansion full of such beautiful art. What an extraordinary frame it gave Rembrandt! I remembered going with Margaret to a special exhibition on jolly old Frans Hals at the Met—and how wonderful it was, really for the first time in my life, to share what I loved with someone who was really getting it—not someone, like my poor mother, who paled with worry when I so much as reached for an art book. This peace came from inside: it was rooted in a new, profound permission not only to love the art I'd always loved but to love myself. I now knew I didn't have to run away from myself anymore—I didn't have to defend or explain anything to anybody! I learned that happiness depended on shamelessly *enjoying* who you were! This was life-changing news.

"And how this changed my stuff with my family! That Christmas was amazing!"

RESOLVING CONFLICT—PEACE AS A MEANS, NOT AN END

When Doreen returned to her family that Christmas, she had had the better part of a month (since she'd seen that column of white light in the woods) of enjoying her work again in the ways she used to enjoy it—with her old irrepressible enthusiasm, her passionate critical eye and imagination.

Now she couldn't quite remember why she'd been so upset when her brother sniped at her over the turkey. Hadn't he simply been a brat again? Why should that have sent her over the edge? When Doreen launched once again into a description of her current art projects, she was met with some of the same grunts and groans and "that's nice, dear"s she'd gotten at Thanksgiving. But for some reason she wasn't upset this time around. She didn't feel hurt, defensive, or dismissed. Actually what she felt like doing—and did—was burst out laughing! Her brother (who'd been poised to attack with another of his "stuck-up sister" salvos) gaped at her. "What are *you* laughing about?" he said, trying unsuccessfully to keep from laughing himself. "Oh, I don't know," Doreen said, catching her breath. And at first she didn't either. But then at least a quasi-explanation burbled out of her (another laugh about to erupt): "It just strikes me as funny that we all can't help being ourselves."

Secure in her own self-acceptance, Doreen's warm, humorous, and loving embrace of her family, welcoming their foibles as well as their strengths, more than marked progress for her. She says that she learned a kind of stance—the first knowledge of which she completely credits to that moment communing with the light in the woods—that she now, twenty years later, brings to everything in her life. "I never realized how fertile the peace that comes from knowing and not fighting yourself, loving yourself, is. I never realized how much good work it can help you get done! And now the idea of 'keeping the peace'—well, that's what this angel helps me to do. Keep the peace *within myself*—keep it alive, keep conscious of it, keep enjoying it, keep relying on it, keep trusting it."

Making reference to angels is still fairly new for Doreen—for a long time she resisted the idea. But now, over two decades past that transformative moment in the woods, after going through the recent deaths of both her parents, dealing now with her younger sister's drug addiction, helping to put her brother through grad school— Doreen's sense of guidance, which she was first conscious of receiving in the woods, has intensified and seems more concrete, specific. She now even finds herself speaking to the "guides" she feels are always with her—guides whose messages or urgings seem to come more often as articulate phrases. "Maybe I've just learned to make myself more available to their guidance," Doreen says. "I do feel like this is due to some growing receptivity in me. Of course I didn't do anything to cultivate it past just relaxing, letting go." When I told her about the progression of angels, she grinned like a Cheshire cat. "I knew that!" She has, in her own way and at her own pace, allowed these angels and their gifts to transform her life.

"But the biggest gift for me is that wonderful, generative peace—that sense that peace is eternally inside me, that it's not something I have to scramble outside of myself to find—the certainty that it won't go away." Doreen smiled a bit, then came out with something her Irish grandmother might have said: "It's almost like I've got a bit of heaven inside me. Does that sound absurd? But that's true: *a bit of eternity inside me.* That's really what it feels like. And from that changeless state of peace, I find I make some pretty good decisions, or at any rate seem to be better at taking advantage of some pretty darned good luck. I got this teaching job at a time when no one was hiring college professors. I love the school, and they're paying me to do postgraduate work—sending me to Holland and Belgium next fall. You know what the feeling is? *I'm being embraced by life.* It's almost as if nothing *could* happen but an embrace, given what"—Doreen smiles self-consciously as she prepares to say the unfamiliar words—"the Angel of Peace has done for me."

Remember that when Doreen returned home at Christmas, she began hearing the same disgruntled sounds of boredom and hostility she'd heard (and been devastated by) at Thanksgiving. Think how she reacted the first time: she lost all interest in a realm—art—that once brought her her greatest pleasures and focus and identity; she felt chaotic and abandoned, as gutted out and empty as that fallen tree in the woods.

But then, at Christmas, she couldn't even remember how she'd felt back at Thanksgiving. She was laughing now! What had changed? She had received the gift of "peace"—the peace of self-acceptance. She discovered the profound truth that we are most secure in the world when we know, accept, and love who we are. This doesn't mean that everyone else is going to know, accept, and love us, too. Doreen heard more than a few grumbles from her father about this "art nonsense," saw more than a few glazed smiles from her mother (who secretly hoped Doreen would put more energy into finding a husband than into art), and definitely fielded more than a few nasty jabs from her fifteen-year-old brother (so full of exploding hormones it was a wonder he wasn't throwing cherry bombs instead). Doreen could *laugh* now. She could feel compassion now. She no longer registered these family reactions as attack. She registered them as evidence of her family *being itself.* She was also more able to respond to the love, now that she was no longer defending herself against what she had projected was the lack of it.

Now more than twenty years later, what lesson sticks most with her? "When you love," she says simply, "love comes back at you." So, she's discovering, does peace. Radiate self-acceptance (whose product is peace), and something gets passed on that's at least a little contagious. When you're around someone who likes himself, you generally find you like yourself better, too. (This stuff is catching.) You will even look better. In fact, when a client complains of not being pretty or handsome enough, my first prayer is to the Angel of

Peace, to bestow the kind of self-love and -acceptance that always translates into visible beauty. I recently had some photographs taken by a photographer I hadn't seen in six years. She wrote me when she sent me the finished pictures: "I didn't recognize you! How'd you get so young and good-looking?" This was flattering but really had nothing to do with me. It was a testament to the calm that the Angel of Peace has helped me to cultivate. Our faces reflect our souls. The more peaceful one is, the more peaceful the other will be.

Peace turns out to be a different animal, perhaps, than you may have thought. It is full of aliveness. It animates you at the same time it helps you to accept and love yourself. True peace is not earned through conflict—something you can only achieve after a war. Peace proceeds from letting go. Peace *resolves* conflict.

This concept of peace goes against some strong received notions: that peace is the *goal* of conflict resolution, not the means of achieving it. Peace is believed to follow war; a kind of initially exhausted state of surrender, a giving-up after a conflict can go no further. Peace is something you fight for. Isn't that what war—at least war that is held to be noble—is all about? One side dukes it out with the other until one is the clear winner, and (if the other is a graceful loser), well—a kind of "peace" is achieved, isn't it?

Not the kind that lasts. Not the kind that heals.

Peace, to the angel who offers it to us, is a live, warm, reassuring, eternal embrace, as necessary to our souls as oxygen is to our lungs. It is a continual letting go, not a giving up. It's not some sort of soporific, like a spiritual sleeping pill. This kind of "live" peace can be a means of settling disputes. When Doreen didn't react defensively, angrily, or tearfully to her family—when she startled them all by laughing!—she demonstrated peace's power to heal, to forestall a fight. Once again, it is not the power of white-knuckled exertion—a kind of stand-off in the middle of a tense tug-of-war. Just as there's no fear in love, there's no fear in peace: it's as free and flowing as a river. It fosters a state of *being*, not doing. Our TAB acronym comes to mind yet again: *Take Action Being*. This is precisely what true peace does for us: acquaints us with our "being"—with who we are simply because we exist—and then helps us choose what to do in the context of our "being," in the context of self-acceptance and peace. By allowing our actions to proceed from the "being," peace is so much simpler an enterprise than most of us were taught. *(Psst: Don't tell anybody, but life doesn't have to be so hard.)*

"A little bit of heaven inside me. A little bit of eternity." These are Doreen's words, describing how peace makes her feel inside. Now, with the Angel of Victory, we'll tug a good deal more of that "heaven," of that "eternity" into the light, into our lives.

Actually, it's more a matter of seeing that it's already here.

9
THE ANGEL OF VICTORY

So many assumptions and ideas begin to change their meanings when we let angels into our lives. Think back to the words we've explored in these pages, words many of us once took for granted. *Vision, wisdom, purity, strength, love,* and *peace*...do you understand them a little differently than you used to?

You now know that vision is deeper and wider than the product of some simple "visualization" exercise: with the Angel of Vision's help, you connect to a clearer picture not only of what you want in life but of who you are and how what you want meshes with your deepest identity. Your vision is immediate and instantly accessible: you respond best to it when you see it as already manifest. It's not some "future" possibility to yearn for—it's what can be (and on some level, *is*) right now.

Wisdom isn't some passive state of looking "wisely" on human affairs from a distance: in angelic terms, it's a practical insight—wisdom suggests a plan of "right action." You learn from it precisely how to manifest your vision. Vision alone is air: with wisdom, it becomes flesh.

Purity is a cleansing shower on that "flesh"—it's the gift of being able to stay true to the *heart* of your vision, to the most important and happiest parts of what you want from it. It helps you toss out anything extraneous or ego-bound in the pursuit of your goals.

Strength is the spiritual stamina to continue on the road that purity has clarified for you. It's not some white-knuckled exertion of power over circumstances: it's the infinite energy that runs through all things and is always accessible and available, giving you whatever resources you need to persist.

The gift of love comes precisely when you need it—when your angelic dream-to-reality "mechanism" is in place and you truly are able now to manifest what you want. This is when you most need to be reminded of the larger aims and the deeper pleasures of the vision you are bringing to life. Love wants to *pour in* at this point; and if you let it, the rewards of the angelic gifts you have so far amassed are likely to increase geometrically. Love lightens and connects, immeasurably enhancing your pleasure in the world and in other people.

Peace follows this flood of love not as some sleep-inducing balm but as the wonderful gift and product of your having *come* to love: yourself and those around you. It's the gift of feeling secure in who you are, able gladly to embrace what you have discovered are your gifts, your role in the world, the positive effects you can have on other people's lives.

There's an angelic "spin" on each of these words and ideas that animates them—makes them memorable and powerful in ways that probably wouldn't have occurred to you if you'd offered your own definitions of each of them at the start of this book. Out of these angelically redefined terms come three simple ideas:

1. You can always reach out for help, which is always infinitely available to you.
2. You deserve what you desire.
3. You are not alone—everything you do in this life is a collaborative effort with others.

This last idea—that we are not alone, that we *participate* in the Universe, we are not apart from it—brings us to the essence of the Angel of Victory.

COURAGE, NOT BRAVERY— VICTORY MEANS TRUST

Remember back in Chapter 2 when I told you about Grace who, at 37, was jobless and nearly hopeless when she came to me? I said then that I asked her to let go of everything she had ever learned in the past—to calm her mind and connect to the higher forces within her. It turned out she was battling an internalized "tape" of her mother berating her, telling her she wasn't pretty or smart or competent enough. She so yearned for release from this "tape" that she was eager and able to "let go." She simply needed the permission to do so that I had offered her.

This is the kind of stuff psychotherapists deal with daily, but most of them would probably say that telling Grace "to let go of everything she had ever learned in the past" is woefully insufficient advice. How can you "let go" of a lifetime of psychic damage simply because someone asks you to? Surely something as deeply rooted as this woman's problems would take weeks, months, even years on the couch to resolve.

I have no gripe with psychotherapists: they help many people face and deal with many different kinds of problems. But angels tell us that we can be released from our bonds anytime we want to. It's the "wanting to" that's important. This isn't some Pollyanna response to human misery. Rather, it's a testament to the power of the state of grace (a phrase Grace loves for obvious reasons!) to which each of us has access simply by asking—asking like a child for help. Grace wasn't "cured" of her internalized mother's scolding so much as she was given the gift of knowing what to do when these self-lacerating criticisms boiled up in her. She could let them pass. She could meditatively seek a "higher" state of being where she would not be hurt by them—because she would know, with the gift of release she had asked for, that they weren't true. She truly wanted the release, and the angelic help she received showed her, instantly, how to attain it.

Knowing this—that we can transcend even the most painful legacies of our backgrounds, shed even the heaviest baggage of our pasts—is the first sign that we've partaken of the gift that the Angel of Victory offers us. We normally think of "victory" as conquering something, overcoming some great frightening foe in a brave fight. The problem with this interpretation is twofold. First, it presupposes that you're alone in the battle: just you and the big bad foe. Second, "brave" suggests you have to stand up to something fearful—or more to the point, you have to overcome your *own* fear in order to win, in order to achieve "victory."

But by the time you are ready to encounter the Angel of Victory, you know that fear is an illusion. Bravery is no longer required.

Courage may be required—but remember the root of the word *courage* is *heart.* Courage acquaints us with trust. We are courageous when we reconnect with love, with the power of the heart, to trust that even when we cannot foresee the outcome, we will benefit by taking the actions our "higher" selves—and our angelic guides—encourage us to take. Courage can be—ultimately always is—joyful. Bravery always is in some clenched measure a response to fear. And fear is a lie.

Remember my parenthetical remark toward the end of the last chapter *(Psst: Don't tell anybody, but life doesn't have to be so hard)?* Well, the Angel of Victory would like you to take out the parentheses. "Victory" means realizing that your passage through life, your journey to happiness, can be, ought to be, very simple. All you have to do is ask for guidance, trust in the response, be courageous (in the heartful sense of the word) in taking the "right actions," and enjoy the ride.

THE ANGELIC ALLIANCE

The first supposition of bravery—that you're all alone fighting a formidable foe—is one that, by the time the Angel of Victory enters your life, you will know without having to be told is a great falsehood.

With the Angel of Victory, you become—you know that you are—a participant in life. If you make conscious contact with this angel, you often experience the presence of many different angels of Victory, symbolizing the many victories of understanding you will have made. You now know what the "rules" are for living the life you want to live, for attaining everything you desire, for connecting to others. But most importantly, you know you're not alone, that what comes to you always involves the participation of your angels, of other people in your life, and of your own "higher power," however you may define it.

A well-known actor I worked with who had known great prominence in a weekly dramatic series but was left professionally stranded when that series ended is a model of "victory." He was and is a very spiritual person—which is to say, he's always been connected to a sense that he's an important participant in the Universe and that everything happens for a reason, even if he may not have a clue what that reason is. By accepting what life handed him—even if it looked like "failure" to others (the cancellation of his series)—he just expected what, in fact, he got: another door opened. He was invited to teach at a community college and run its drama department. He'd never taught before and had always wanted to. He wasn't bothered by the supposed lack of prestige—it wasn't Yale, by any means. But he saw it as a wonderful opportunity. The school put him up in a charming old Victorian house that was perfect for his family. His two young sons were happy as puppies—the place had a huge yard and lots of kids for neighbors. His wife, a social worker, was able to get work quickly in a nearby clinic, working with homeless kids— something she'd always wanted to do. Papa the actor threw himself into his teaching, and very soon he had one of the leading drama departments in his portion of the state. People came from far and wide to see his productions.

Ultimately my friend shifted slightly in his career—a producer was so impressed by his understanding of acting, which had obviously generatively informed decisions he made as a director, that he offered the actor/director a chance to take over directing an independent film that was then on the rocks. He eagerly accepted the opportunity—with the same courageous, childlike embrace he'd brought to everyone and every aspect of his life—and he was once again "victorious."

We are in alliance with each other when we are victorious. We know that our "successes" are not all our own doing. But we are in partnership with something greater, too—and this, probably, is what the Angel of Victory wants us to take joy in most: we are in alliance with God.

10

HEAVEN ON EARTH
A Meditation

While I can't anticipate all of the questions you've still got, I probably can anticipate a few. For example, often in this book I've talked about making contact, through meditation, with your angels—whether "guardian" or one of the seven categories to which this book has mainly been devoted. But what exactly am I talking about? How *do* you contact these beings?

First, don't forget what we learned at the outset: you don't have to experience some "vision" of an angel to be helped by an angel or even to feel an angel's presence. The first suggestion is always to act "as if." Amazing things will happen if you never get further than that.

The problem about teaching you how to achieve a meditative state is that it can't really be taught—at least not out of a book. In fact, even in the presence of someone who has a track record of being able to help people relax and achieve the kind of "alpha" state of receptivity that allows them to "hear" their angels, even that won't work if you're fundamentally resistant. The point is, nobody can do it for you—which is not the same thing as saying you have to do it alone. (Indeed, you can't do it alone—meditating always means connecting spiritually with a higher power.) But you do have to *want* to "let go," as Grace wanted (and thus was able) to "let go."

All I can do is what I have done: tell you what I know, and pass on what these angels have so eagerly shared with me.

Including the following meditation, the words of which I have passed on to hundreds of people, sometimes singly, sometimes in groups. They offer a kind of sum-up of our angels, an overview of what they eternally want us to know. The meditation is as close to verbatim "channeling" as you'll find in this book—although everything here has come as a gift, sieved through my own abilities to receive and transmit it, from angelic sources. This meditation is something I'd urge you to read aloud, to yourself. Don't struggle over it: just read it. It's not poetry. It's not even an obvious prayer. It's just me passing on to you what the angels tell me.

It will help you, I think, to open the gates a little wider to the loving power of these angels—beings whose existence is given meaning only when you accept the gifts they so long to bestow.

HEAVEN ON EARTH: A MEDITATION

Angels are always working with us. Most people have had experiences with them even if they don't know it. The seven creative angels are planks on the bridge to your happiest life.

Get comfortable. Clear your mind. Focus on the desire you'd like to share with your angels or guides. Choose a word, if you'd like, to keep distractions from your mind. Breathe deeply, clear away all thoughts. Sit back, relax. Let the energy flow through your body. Feel yourself becoming lighter, lifting your vibration and spirit. As you emerge, rising above your body, start to feel the

separation of your energy—leave your body, allow your energy to rise to a higher level.

You are now floating, floating through the clouds. Just leaving your worries. Your day. Your job. Your friends. Just feel the energy floating through the sky, the clouds, through which you float so effortlessly. Floating. Pillows of light. Vibrating with your energy. As you float, you will see two gates that are waiting to open to you, greet you. Acknowledge this opening, love it, accept it, move toward it. As the gates open, you will see two angels waiting to meet you. Acknowledge them. Love them. Accept them. The gates are opening. Fly into their secret world. As you float, you see clouds and blue sky. As you enter the next area, you see a big white marble door. The door is opening. Go inside.

As you enter, you will see your Angel of Vision. This angel will give you sight. Release all the negative things you have seen as a child and as an adult. Just release them at the door. Let the angel bathe you in the energy and vision around you. Feel the presence around you. Feel the love. Feel the light. Now take the angel's vision with you as you float out the door and the door closes. You are floating to the next level. You are flying effortlessly.

The next door appears—opens. The Angel of Wisdom is there to greet you. Step inside, and let go of all negative thoughts, doubts, resistance. Let it flow out of you. Just release it. The Angel of Wisdom surrounds you with light. This angel offers you the wisdom of centuries—the wisdom of knowing that you are perfect in life. Right now. The wisdom to know that you can create what you want in this life. Greet your angel. Thank him. Float out. Let the

door close. Now you are floating to the next level. The level is higher—you feel lifted up. The Angels of Vision and Wisdom accompany you to the third door. It opens.

The Angel of Purity now greets you. Float in to greet this angel. Let this angel bathe you with pure love, helping you to release further negativity, giving you clarity. You are now free of any discordant vibrations. You are cleansed. Energy, vitality, healing, and comfort all flood into you. Thank this angel. Let this door close. Float to the next level. You are now a powerful individual as you ascend to a higher level.

Another door appears: the Angel of Strength opens it wide for you. Enter. Greet your angel. Let the power of the Universe bathe you, heal you. Acknowledge that this is happening. Let this light fill you completely. Thank your angel, and float out of the door. Move on to the next level. As you float higher, your consciousness becomes clearer. Your vision is in complete harmony with your life.

You see the next door. It opens. You meet the Angel of Love. Enter. Feel the presence of unlimited love. Embrace this angel with all your heart and soul. The love bathes you more completely than you ever thought possible. Let the safety, the comfort of that love inside you. Accept this love. Say "Thank you. I accept that love now. I am that love." Just float in love. Thank the angel as you depart. Carry that love with you always. The door closes, and you go up one more level. As you enter the next level, there is an even larger door. It opens.

The Angel of Peace appears. Let this angel bathe you in peace, for your body, for your mind. The comfort of peace is all around you—it energizes you as it calms you. Let the vibration of peace enter and fill you. Now come out, and let the door close. Thank this angel. Move to the next door. It opens. There are many angels here to greet you.

These are the Angels of Victory. They tell you that you have attained many victories, including victory within yourself. You have accomplished everything you set out to do. You have attained what you wanted in your life. You have accepted everything that is within you. You realize that you are not alone, that you are an important participant in the Universe. You know that you are loved. As you say good-bye to all of them, thank them, and be glad that you have won their love.

Float out of the door as it closes. You are now heading toward the front gates, where the first angels greeted you. You have their gifts inside you: vision, wisdom, purity, strength, love, peace, and victory. Accept these—accept that they are yours. Say good-bye to your guides at the front. Bask in their love for you as you exit the gates.

You are floating, lighter, brighter. The gates are closing. You are floating with all this knowledge and power and love. You are an incredible individual who possesses everything you need. As you float through the clouds, find where home is. See that space or circle in the clouds. It is time to come back to your body, back to the earth. The earth body is connected to the ethereal body. You now know they are one. Everything you have learned on this journey you will take with you. You will always have this information. You will be illuminated. Your energy will radiate. You can *create everything you need whenever you need it. Just enter your body slowly. Thank your angels for the fabulous journey they have taken you on. Stay connected. Feel the energy. Your angels are with you always. Feel them. Use them. They have helped you to create heaven on earth.*

ANGELS
A Quick Guide

Simple Facts, Questions and Answers
Prayers to Access Angels
Daily Journal and Workbook

SIMPLE FACTS, QUESTIONS AND ANSWERS

WHAT ARE ANGELS?

Angels are the "wires" of the Universe—they afford us a means of spiritual communication that we can access in no other way. Above all, they are messengers. They don't have opinions; they have no free will. They are completely realized beings with a single focus: to help us grow and thrive materially and spiritually. They will take any form that maximizes the effectiveness of the message. They may sometimes resemble human beings, communicate through a tune or song lyric, produce a sweet and evocative scent, whisper suggestions or instructions, or create in your mind's eye an image they know you want to see. The particular temperament and personality of the recipient determine how angels communicate and what form they may take. They want to convey precisely what they know you will understand best, in the ways you most yearn to see or receive it.

 But because we're beginners in the spirit world—largely uninformed about spiritual manifestations, not always able to decipher or make them out—we can't always see (because we have not been trained to "see") what our angels are revealing. Probably the best way to prepare yourself for an angelic messenger is to shed as many expectations as you can. For example, did you ever turn on the radio and hear exactly the song you wanted to hear?

An angel might have rigged it.

WHAT ARE GUARDIAN ANGELS, AND HOW DO I CONNECT WITH MINE?

Guardian angels are exactly what their name suggests: angels whose job it is to guard, protect, and guide us. Often they are the little voice you hear inside your head—sometimes perceived as conscience, sometimes suggesting a creative solution to a particularly bothersome problem, sometimes warning you not to say or do something dangerous. Guardian angels will push you to do things they know it's time for you to do; sometimes they will lead you to places they know you need to go. Attempt to access them through prayer and meditation, but do not be disappointed if they resist appearing: they work with you in tried and true ways, and if they've succeeded over time in persuading you to take positive action, there may be no need for them to materialize. Sometimes—as when the Archangel Michael appeared to me—a guardian angel may take visible form or in some other way seek a more dramatic impact. This is always because they have something particularly important to convey—an insight or message deemed to be crucial for you at that particular point in your life. Remember, you don't have to seek the counsel of your guardian angel to obtain it: your angel will make sure you "get the message." Of course, the more psychically receptive you become, the clearer that message will be. Cultivate that openness and receptivity through meditation, and you'll make sure the gateway stays wide open.

Why Do Angels Come to Us?

Souls resonate with each other in almost musical ways. Certain vibrations mesh more easily with certain other vibrations—and the effect is a kind of mutual magnetism. There is always harmonic synchrony between angels and the souls of the people they guide, serve, inform. Any angel with whom you have contact will always "vibrate" in sync with your own energy, so that when you ask for an angel's help, you send out a form of energy that attracts similar energy back. This is why there's *always* a perfect fit between you and whatever angel has come to you.

How Do We Call Angels to Us?

First of all, angels are always here. But whatever prayer, meditation, or ritual comfortably feels like it's opening you up will work just fine. There is no right or wrong way to contact angels. Remember, they are spiritual "phone wires"—they leap at the opportunity to act as conduits for the messages they know you need. The genuine desire for their presence and help is enough to get those angelic wires buzzing. Open up, and they'll come to you.

Can a Person Be an Angel and Not Know It?

No. An angel is not a human being, and no human being can become an angel—with only one exception documented in spiritual history

PRAYERS TO ACCESS ANGELS

This section offers specific suggestions for accessing each of the seven angels we've explored in this book. But first review the following general guidelines. They will help you to become more optimally receptive—enabling whatever angel whose help you seek to contact you more clearly and completely.

- ✓ Learn how to let information flow through you.
- ✓ Ask your angels to come forth and teach you the stillness of knowing your being is powerful.
- ✓ Use words with positive vibrations (reflecting your higher, most loving self and freest, most embracing aspirations).
- ✓ Speak in the present tense—*now.*
- ✓ Give yourself permission to go forward.
- ✓ Listen for the message.

A PRAYER TO SAY BEFORE YOU SEEK AN ANGEL'S HELP

Beloved Almighty: I am present. I command you to keep me, reminding me always to acknowledge you first in everything that I do, and when I accomplish something successfully, see that I give the recognition to the angelic hosts who at the inner ... are always assisting me in every constructive activity of ...fe. I accept my life as constant perfection.

and lore. Metatron was said to be the head of all the angels—a sort of "top" archangel. He was Enoch in human form: in ancient times he reached 300 years, and God took him and made his *nefesh*—his soul—into an angel. He ascended into the "99 percent"—a spiritual realm in which he never left a cell of his body but exists also as energy. His assumption into this realm and his soul's transformation into an angel are the first and only record of this happening.

IS THERE ANY REASON TO BE CAUTIOUS ABOUT ANGELS?

As you learned in this book, angels are pure positive energy—they exist completely to relay life-affirming messages. If you encounter a spiritual presence that disturbs you or conveys negativity, it is almost certainly the departed soul of a human being in transition from this realm to the next.

But when you learn various names of angels—such as the nar the Archangels Michael, Gabriel, Urial, and Rafael—or nar your guardian angels may have revealed to you, it's wise ful of saying them without intending their namesake ar An angel's name is a powerful way to beckon to them have no free will, and they will come when called, ' occasions, when you're not prepared for the' "rock" you a bit—not unlike receiving too m? tion. Think their names, but it's a good id out loud if you don't really require the'

CONTACTING THE ANGELS OF VISION, WISDOM, PURITY, STRENGTH, LOVE, PEACE, AND VICTORY

As you recite the following in-the-now affirmations, visualize yourself speaking with your angel as you would speak to your best friend. Listen for the response, then take action.

The Angel of Vision

✓ I now invite the Angel of Vision into my life.

✓ I receive all the messages and ask for the help of this angel.

✓ I am acting "as if," creating what it is that I want in this life. Without fear, I take action.

✓ I ask this guide to light my path.

✓ I give thanks for my life and am grateful for my Angel of Vision within.

The Angel of Wisdom

✓ I now invite my Angel of Wisdom to help me with information that I require, and I gratefully receive it.

✓ My life is filled with unlimited wisdom.

✓ The wisdom gives me strength to create something new in my life—a new relationship or career.

✓ The Angel of Wisdom takes away old ideas or unhelpful "tapes" that keep playing in my head.

✓ I ask that this angel guide me safely along my spiritual path.

✓ I am an electric light force of wisdom that attracts creative ideas and enables them to flow through me.

✓ I give thanks for my life and am grateful for my Angel of Wisdom within.

The Angel of Purity

✓ I surrender to the Angel of Purity who brings me clear and positive energies.

✓ I welcome this wave of deep cleansing of my soul.

✓ I let this angel work with me to forgive everything that is causing any emotional confusion around myself.

✓ I open my body to the pure cool healing energy that this angel gives to me.

✓ I choose to become whole and pure in my everyday thoughts.

✓ I let pure miracles happen in my life.

✓ I give thanks for my life and am grateful for my Angel of Purity within.

The Angel of Strength

✓ I choose to attract an abundance of new ideas and positive people in my life.

✓ I have an unlimited flow of energy that my Angel of Strength continues to nourish.

✓ It is easy for me to make important decisions in my life.

✓ My guide is giving me spiritual energy every day.

✓ I use my Angel of Strength to assist and enhance others that need help in their lives.

✓ My Angel of Strength gives me the trust within.

✓ I give thanks for my life and am grateful for my Angel of Strength within.

The Angel of Love

✓ My Angel of Love opens my heart to the divine power.

✓ I am energy of God, masters, and angels that are in me.

✓ I am radiating constant love and abundance.

✓ My relationships are from the highest good.

✓ I am seeing the love within each person in my life.

✓ I open my heart so that this angel may simply float through me. I notice how it feels to receive the love and support of this angel.

✓ I expand myself by telling several close friends how much I love them.

✓ I celebrate my love for myself by doing something really nice for me, something I would not ordinarily do.

✓ I give thanks for my life and am grateful for my Angel of Love within.

The Angel of Peace

✓ I ask my guides always to surround me in their presence.

✓ I always feel comfort about my life; my guide gives me inner quietness within my body, mind, and soul.

✓ My guardian Angel of Peace always guides me to the best peaceful situations in life.

✓ I am always safe, protected, and loved.

✓ I am a magnet to peace that exists within all situations.

✓ There is always balance in my life.

✓ I give thanks for my life and am grateful for my Angel of Peace within.

The Angel of Victory

✓ I ask my guide to give me only the best in life.

✓ My angels watch over me while I sleep.

✓ I ask my angels to illuminate my bright light.

✓ I ask my angels to bring hope to other people.

✓ I am inspired throughout my journey.

✓ I call upon my Angel of Victory to be in my intention in everything I do.

✓ I act as if I am a winner.

✓ I expect that I have it already.

✓ I always speak higher vibrational thoughts about others.

✓ I build on my success.

✓ I choose to be rich and happy.

✓ I know that my talents and abilities are the best.

✓ I give thanks for my life and am grateful for my Angel of Victory within.

DAILY JOURNAL AND WORKBOOK

This daily journal and workbook are provided to help you create the life you want. Angels are full of inspiration and beacons of light: they are always around us. Asking your guides and angels for help, using what you have learned or experienced up to this point, you are now ready for dramatic, fundamental change and growth.

Let's go deeper to find more clarity about your magnificent, unfolding self. There are no "right" answers or responses to any of the questions, suggestions, and partial statements you will see here.

Your answers will be based on what is true for you, on your own personal system of beliefs. What works for you may not work for someone else, which is why we must trust our inner guides to take us to those places within that are purely our own.

Before we start, I ask you to open yourself up and repeat this declaration three times aloud:

My life is wonderful! I am being healed and accept all guidance that is given to me. My requests are fulfilled by divine action for the highest good. I now accept these gifts of abundance, joy, peace, and health—now!

So that you are in complete harmony with your spiritual self, I will now direct you to participate in a contract with your higher guides. Signing this contract signifies your commitment to change or tune up your awareness in life. Remember it is never too late to change. You can be reborn at any time. Every moment is the beginning of new life. We all have the power of choice. Angels simply activate this power—or communicate to us its presence and accessibility.

READ THIS CONTRACT ALOUD, ENTER YOUR NAME AT THE LINE AT THE TOP, AND SIGN WHERE INDICATED AT THE BOTTOM:

I, _____, am now trusting myself and my higher guides to give me the information that I require to create my heaven on earth. I am making my choices about what feels right and good inside me. All my special talents and all the information I need are flowing within me. I am honoring myself by loving everyone around me. Every day I accept a miracle in my life. I let go of old thoughts and patterns, and let my angelic guides activate everything around me. I live in the *now* and celebrate my magnificence.

Your signature _____

Date _____

You'll now begin to explore specifically what your true desires are in life. Keep the following general points in mind as you reflect on what you want your life to be.

✓ Do not judge by appearances.
✓ You are not trapped in the material world.
✓ You are not your bank account, fame, or job.
✓ Angel spirit guides are eternally accessible.
✓ Unify with this power and accept it.
✓ Love yourself and your body.
✓ Take the risk to be who you really are.

✓ Be grateful and humble.

Your Wishes, Goals, and Desires

Consult your higher self about what you most truly want to create, as well as the area or realm (spirituality, finances, relationships, music, physical well-being, work, and so on) it will involve. Ask for angelic guidance and then fill in the blank spaces below.

My Desire and Wish Are to Be:

My Desire and Wish Are to Do:

My Desire and Wish Are to Have:

These next exercises will help you to get even more specific and focused about your true purpose. (Remember that the operative word and idea throughout this series of exercises is *permission*.) Connect with your higher self, ask for angelic guidance, and then complete these partial statements in the blank spaces beneath them:

If I did not have to worry about finances, I would:

If I did not have to worry about my age, I would:

My perfect romantic partner and soul mate would have, be, do, and look like the following (describe in complete physical, emotional, spiritual, and mental detail):

FOR YOUR (AND YOUR ANGELS') EYES ONLY

Seventeen Questions that will:

Give You Focus,

Open You to New Possibilities,

Change Old Assumptions,

Increase Self-Awareness

Invite Angelic Guidance,

and Help You to Create a New Life

Answer the following questions as candidly as you can. Write down the first impressions or reactions that occur to you. Don't edit yourself. Don't worry about other people's reactions. This questionnaire concerns no one but you. The more honest your responses, the clearer you will be about the life you yearn to live and the person you dream of being—and how, with angelic help, you can make them reality now.

1. What don't I like about my body or my physical appearance?

2. What would my ideal body and physical appearance be like?

3. What problems am I encountering with my career?

4. What are my ideal career conditions, and what results do I expect from these conditions?

5. What problems or situations can I identify that are blocking me at this time?

6. What are the ideal solution(s) to these problems? What would unblock all difficulty and allow things to flow?

7. What are my spiritual beliefs?

8. What do I expect from my angels?

9. *What doubts do I have that angels really exist? Although I may never have seen one, what would an angel look like if I did see one?*

10. *What will people think or say if I let them know that I believe in angels or have had a personal experience with an angel or angels?*

11. *What do I expect from myself?*

12. *Why do I have difficulty trusting and loving everyone in my life?*

13. *Why am I angry? Am I holding on to resentments from any-one in my life? If so who, and what did he/she/they do to me—how was I hurt?*

14. *I write down below the names of all people who hurt me or whom I could not forgive for their behavior toward me. I forgive them, bless them, and release them with love.*

15. What do I expect in other people?

16. What are the seven things I am great at?

- _____
- _____
- _____
- _____
- _____
- _____
- _____

17. What are the seven things I love about myself?

- _____
- _____
- _____
- _____
- _____
- _____
- _____

You are now ready to live the life you want. Create the change today. Use your higher self and your angels to lift your spirits. Use your power to create your greatness today. Take the risk to be who you are. Know that you are eternally loved and blessed.

ACKNOWLEDGMENTS

In creating this project, I would like to acknowledge the following loving spirits who have made my journey into this work a loving and ongoing trusting experience. Also the many family, friends, clients, and special people whom I have had the privilege to know or work with along this incredible path.

First and foremost, this book could not have been written without the professional help of the amazing Guy Kettelhack, an extraordinary writer and renaissance man whose true spirit is now shining bright!

Many blessings and thanks to my mother and father.

Thank you, Barbara Moulton, my agent, for your trust, strength, and friendship.

For the birth of this project, and for vision: thank you, Patricia Gift and Linda Loewenthal. (And thanks, to the wonderful copyeditor Janet Biehl.)

Special thanks to the following people: Evelyn M. Dalton, Deborah A. Luican, Patty Q, Martin Allaire, Nastassja Kinski, Gina Webb, Ute-Ville, Utta, Dottie Galliano, Nance Mitchell, Ani, Billy Blanks, Anne Taylor Spitzer, Elena Sahagun, Mel Harris, Carole Dib, Mahie Mahboubi, Laa Joshua, Kate Bolyn, Maggy Calhoun, Donna Mills, SEAL, Teri Garr, Linda Gray, Pamela Deans-Levine, Harold Lancer, Hilary Barrett, Mary Griffin, Michael Westhofen, Donna Delory, Bruce R. Hatton, Shelly Burton, Sante Losio, Doriana Mazzola,

Acknowledgments

John Travolta, Sylvia Castillo, Barbara Deutsch, Vincent Schiavelli, Sara Anne Fox, Lori Goldman, Carol Campbell, Nina Paolucci, Marilu Henner, Myriam Calhoun, Ralf Bauer, Antoinette Kuritz, David Newman, Mary Ann Viterbo, Gry Eriksen, Laura Galinson, Liz Caldwell, Katarina Witt, Elaine Moyle (Toronto Sun), Kelly Knight, Ryan Doyle (CFRB Radio, Toronto), Dana Dugan, Denise Fierro, Jonelle Allen, Richard Cole, R.Q., George Maimon, Cheryl Welch, Lucia Moro, Samara Saffian, Herb Tannen, Lynda Beattie, John Maroney, Tina Constable, Sarah Bennie, Sarah Trosper, Joan M. DeMayo, Rhoda Dunn, Pamela Roskin, Kieran O'Brien, Ndidi Nkagbu, Craig Campobasso, Jeena Lee, Pamela Sheppard, Brian Wright, Grace Bean, Iris Loesel, Andreas Kurz, Gena Lee Nolin, Ed Marx, Debbie Koenig, Pat Beh Werblin, Harold Dupre, Dr. David J. Walker, Glenda Bailey, Don Skeoch, Tom Janczur, Damon Miller, WH2O, Marcia Strassman, Lacine Forbes, Velma Cato, Olivier Wilkins, Rachael Taylor, Candace Groskreutz, Claudio Blotta, Rudi Unterthiner, Penny Marshall, Seiko Matsuda, Kavita Daswani, Liza Sullivan, Marina, Marc Henri Caillard, Christina Crowe, Tamar, Victoria, Belinda Di Bene, Paulo Figueiredo, Chip Gibson, Linda Friedman, Sarah, Ivan Kavalsky, and Veronica DeLaurentis.